In Moving Right Along in the Spirit, *Dennis Bennett helps you discover a deeper understanding of God and His will …a more balanced expression of praise and worship… and a more surefooted evaluation of spiritual experiences. He considers questions concerning God's will— when to accept circumstances and when to take authority over them in the name of Jesus. He examines some of the schemes of the enemy that are designed to discredit genuine expressions of the Holy Spirit. And he points out the need to exercise your spiritual freedom with wisdom and love toward fellow believers. Above all, Dennis Bennett encourages you to be open to God's supernatural blessings and, at the same time, to move "at the right pace, in the right direction, at the right time, in the right way." Wherever you are in your Christian walk, you'll learn how to travel a straight and sure path—the key to* Moving Right Along in the Spirit.

Moving Right Along In the Spirit

The Balanced Path to Maturity

Dennis Bennett

Power Books

Fleming H. Revell Company
Old Tappan, New Jersey

Library of Congress Cataloging in Publication Data

Bennett, Dennis J.
  Moving right along in the spirit.

  Bibliography: p.
  1. Christian life—1960–   . 2. Spiritual healing.
I. Title.
BV4501.2.B3925 1983   230'.3   82-11206
ISBN 0-8007-5184-1

This book is lovingly dedicated to my wife
Rita
A wonderful partner and a true friend in Jesus

Acknowledgements

I have dedicated this book to my wife, Rita, because she is the one who with patience, and sometimes endurance, not only loves me, encourages me, feeds me (physically and spiritually), and cares for my welfare in a hundred ways, but also she is an absolutely outstanding copy editor, rewriter, and general all-around essential working partner.

Special thanks to Sue Williams, our secretary, for the many things she does to help in something like this.

Hearty thanks to Janet Biggart, a dear friend, for her encouragement and for the many hours she spent reading over the manuscript.

Loving appreciation to all the friends who have been praying for me and for this book.

Much appreciation to the editorial staff at Fleming Revell, a most pleasant and understanding group to work with.

Glory and praise to the Lord Jesus Christ our Savior, who alone makes it possible for us to "move right along in the Spirit."

Contents

Preface

I was born in England, and in 1965 revisited my native land for the first time in thirty-eight years. Among many exciting experiences, I spent an hour with the Very Reverend Eric Abbott, Dean of Westminster Abbey, in his study, and when we arose to go, he said, "I want to show you something." He led us down through many passages until we emerged into a vaulted room. "This is the Jerusalem Chamber," he said, "where the committee of forty-seven worked to produce the Authorized Version of the Bible." Can you imagine forty-seven people working together, and bringing forth something as uniformly excellent as the King James translation? Can anyone doubt that they were guided by the Spirit of God?

The Scripture quotations used in this book are from the King James Version of the Bible, unless otherwise noted. This isn't for reasons of nostalgia, or because I have a reactionary desire to hang on to the old Book, but because, as far as I can see, nothing has replaced it as the foundational English version. It is often difficult to the modern ear and the language is often archaic. It is not free from errors and mistranslations. It reflects the ethos of Elizabethan monarchy; but it does provide a fixed point of reference amid the many later translations. I'd rather start from King James and do whatever is needed in interpreting, modernizing, explaining, and paraphrasing, than I would let go of it, and just move from modern version to modern version as it suited my fancy. This book is concerned with balance, and I think this is a way to keep our balance with the Scriptures.

It troubles me that so many people don't know the King James Version, that so many people only know the Scripture through one or more of the moderns. I appreciate those: The Jerusalem Bible, The Living Bible, The New English Bible, Moffatt, Goodspeed, and all the rest. They are tremendously helpful and I thank God for them. I wouldn't dissuade anyone from using them, but I admit I would like everyone to be familiar with King James first, and go on from there. Actually I have used other translations, paraphrases, and literal translations as much or more than the Authorized Version, but I believe it needs to be kept in view. I'm still thankful to the illustrious forty-seven who worked in the Jerusalem Chamber to bring forth a miracle of literary grace, the King James Version of the Holy Bible.

As I have already indicated, all Scripture quotations herein are from the King James Version unless otherwise identified. Where words have been modernized, I have indicated it as KJV Mod. Scripture quotations from The Jerusalem Bible are so noted; quotations from The New English Bible are marked NEB. Those quotations paraphrased by the author are marked AP and instances of a literal Greek translation are so noted. Quotations marked "BCP 1928" are taken from *The Book of Common Prayer,* 1928, of the Episcopal Church USA.

It probably is not necessary to point it out, but in this book whenever I speak of "men" or "mankind," I mean "men and women," or "mankind and womankind," the whole human race. We sorely need some new words in the English language to mean both sexes in such contexts. "Human beings" or "human race" grows clumsy.

The same problem faces the writer with pronouns. "He," "him," and "his" are often used in this book when both sexes are indicated, according to the accepted convention of the English language. We don't have a singular pronoun that specifically means both genders, and to use "she" alone is too restrictive.

"He or she," "his or her," "him or her" carried on too long through a paragraph grow wearyingly awkward. We either need to accept the use of "they" and "their" as grammatical in these places, or else someone needs to invent a pronoun that would do for this problem what the word "siblings" does for "brothers and sisters." What about using, say, "le" to replace "he or she," "ler" to stand for "his or her," and "lim," for "him or her?" Is there any language with pronouns that do this? I'm not aware of it, if there is. Who wants to pioneer it?

Writing Books

The problem with writing books is that there never seems to come a point at which one is willing to say, "Okay, that's it!" and send it off to the publisher. One is always aware that there is more to be said, and that it could be said better. This is one of the reasons editors have deadlines! So here is this book. I hope it proves helpful. It doesn't pretend to be a learned work, although I hope I have been scholarly where scholarship is needed. I've tried to make it as straightforward and understandable as I could. I have asked God's blessing and guidance as I've been writing it, and I pray that God will bless and guide you by His Spirit as you read it, helping you remember and profit by what is true and helpful, and forget anything that is not.

In the love of Jesus Christ.

Dennis Bennett
February 17, 1982

Moving Right Along In the Spirit

The Balanced Path to Maturity

1

Introduction

When people are first filled with the Holy Spirit they become aware of God's goodness in a new way: how wonderful and kind and mirthful He is. It sometimes isn't very long, however, before this new joy in God's love begins to be eroded and questioned as older pictures of God crowd it out. That's why this book begins by talking about what God is like. I'd like to remind those who want to "move right along" in the freedom of the Spirit what God has shown them about Himself, that He is a God who loves and desires people to be free to love Him and one another.

The book attempts to illuminate, too, some of the things that are being returned to the people of God, such as healing and praise; to point out some pitfalls and offer answers to some pressing questions, and explain some of the phenomena that puzzle people as they look at the renewal.

The book deals a bit with the question of how people who have discovered new freedom in their Christian lives should conduct themselves in corporate worship.

You will find some "old" subjects here that might seem to have been thoroughly covered before. I think they need to be reviewed, because of erosion that has taken place since the first clear insights of renewal. "Tell me the story often, for I forget so soon."

There is one chapter on an issue which is troubling the Christian community again, creation and evolution. Christians, especially in the United States, need to overcome a persistent image which portrays them as poorly-informed and backward, extremely right-wing in politics, and anti-intellectual in their faith. We need to really "come on strong" at this point, to show that it is only believing in the true God that can bring intelligence in science, beauty in art, and integrity in business and politics. Our society is slowly being destroyed because of the loss of belief. The trend can still be reversed if art, reason, experience, and belief can be brought together in the light of the Holy Spirit. But we need to cooperate with Him.

A Safe Way to Ride

We are talking about "moving right along in the Spirit." We have a spiritual enemy who doesn't want us to have a smooth ride, or to reach our destination. Let's consider how he might try to interfere with us.

Imagine a man who is about to mount his horse and ride to bring an important message to the mayor of the next town. And imagine further that there is someone who wants to stop that message from getting through. How might he, without undue violence, accomplish that?

Right off, he might try to persuade the messenger that horses are dangerous. "My mother saw a man kicked by a horse once—he spent six months in the hospital. And my uncle was bitten by a horse. Nasty animals. I'd stay away from them if I were you!"

But this little plan fails, and the man is determined to mount. So his adversary tries to persuade him to climb into the saddle the wrong way 'round, facing the horse's tail!

The messenger is too smart for this, though, and gets properly seated on the horse's back, his feet in the stirrups, and gathers the reins into his hand. What now?

"Aha!" says the villain, "I'll aim him in the wrong direction! The town he wants to reach is to the south, I'll convince him he should ride north!

"That didn't work! Well, then I'll just stand in his way. I won't let him get past.

"Oops! He almost rode me down, but I've one last trick up my sleeve!"

And as the horse goes by the villain gives him a terrific slap on the flank, so that the animal begins to run wild. "Ah, if only he will keep running like that! If only that horse, when he gets to his destination, will just run like mad through the town; then everyone will think the rider is reckless or crazy, and they won't believe what he has to tell them!"

So the enemy tries to interfere with our journey. He tries to steal good things from us by telling us they're dangerous or wrong. If that fails, he attempts to get us aimed in the wrong direction, to do things from wrong motives. And if we don't fall for that, he just tries to get in the way, to stir up trouble for us if he can. But if all else fails, he tries to get us to go out of control; to be so enthusiastic that we frighten people, and they fail to see that we have something wonderful to tell them.

Let's keep our balance as we move along in the Spirit, at the right pace, in the right direction, at the right time, in the right way.

2

What Is God Like?

My wife Rita, several years after graduating from college, went to a party one evening with a friend. On the way, her escort challenged her, "Did you read in the paper tonight about the terrible fire in that orphanage? If there's a God, as you say there is, how come He let all those little kids get burned up?"

People, you see, take it for granted that if there is a God, He is both good, and all-powerful. Rita's friend reasoned that if God existed, He, being both loving and in full control, would let only good things happen. Since very bad things were happening, it followed that God did not exist.

What about it? Is God good, and is He all powerful? Can He be both at the same time? One man said, "If God is good, He is not God; if God is God, He is not good."

People who believe in God try to account in other ways for the bad things that happen. Some say, "God is all powerful. He controls everything. Everything happens the way He wants it. He makes bad things happen, so He can bring good out of them later."

We were at a meeting several years ago and the chairman told of a local teenage girl who had been terribly injured in an automobile accident and, after some weeks in great pain, had died. She was a real believer, and all through her ordeal had told how much she loved God. The girl's faith and courage stirred the whole town, and some accepted Christ because of it. The chairman told us that God had planned the terrible accident to happen to the girl so that those people would be converted. God had caused that evil, he said, in order to bring the good.

God certainly brings good out of evil. "All things work together for good to them that love God,"[1] that's true, but that doesn't mean God *causes* the "all things." If a terrorist bombs an airport, or sets fire to a building, we consider him a menace to society. The terrorist, however, would say he was doing evil to bring good results—attracting attention to an injustice so it would be corrected. Wouldn't God be behaving like the terrorist, if He caused a disaster so that something good might come of it later? St. Paul said that some people accused him of teaching, "Do evil, that good may come of it."[2] Paul comments that those people should be censured. Do you think, then, that Paul would have agreed that *God* would "do evil, that good may come of it"? I really don't think so!

Others would not go quite so far. They would say, "God doesn't *cause* evil. He's almighty, and everything happens according to His will, but, you see, He has a 'perfect' will and a 'permissive' will. Those orphans got burned up, that girl was injured, wars and hurricanes and earthquakes and all the other bad and destructive things happen according to His *permissive* will. He doesn't *cause* those events; He just *allows* them to take place."

What is the real difference, though, between *permitting* something to happen that you could have prevented, and directly *causing* it to happen? For example, if you know the bridge is out down the road, and you don't warn people, even though you had nothing to do with breaking the bridge, you're still partly responsible for accidents that happen.

Saying that God would cause evil, or intentionally permits bad things to happen, in order to bring good, both result in making people afraid of Him. In a nearby community a little Bible bookstore burned down. It was a crisis for the owner, who had been struggling to build the business for nearly three years, and had no insurance. As reported in the local paper, her first thought was that God had burned her store down! Said she: "I was afraid. I thought, 'Is God on a vengeance streak?' " She felt that from then on she was going to be "walking bent over from fear not knowing where the next blow was coming from." She didn't stay that way long, though. A friend reminded her what God promised in Psalm 112, "The righteous will never be moved; he will be remembered for ever. He is not afraid of evil tidings; his heart is firm, trusting in the Lord."[3] Then, she said, she was no longer afraid, "The Lord took away my fear," and she went on to trust Him to help her rebuild.

But many do, in effect, walk around "bent over," abjectly afraid of God. They see Him as an unpredictable Being who may hurt them at any moment for no reason or cause that they can understand. It's true, as Hebrews 12:6 says, that as a true Father, God corrects and, if necessary, punishes the children He loves when they do wrong; and it's clear that He will let a rebellious or wicked person get into trouble, or cause trouble for him, if necessary, hoping to make him change his ways. But God isn't like a teacher I once had in school in England, who, if a student was misbehaving, would throw the handiest thing on his desk at him and if he missed the offender and hit another boy, would say, "That'll do for next time!" In that class we knew we were going to be punished sooner or later, no matter how well-behaved we tried to be, because the teacher was sadistic and enjoyed hurting people. God is not sadistic, and He doesn't "chastise" His children for nothing, for a whim, or "for next time."

On Providence

Dorothy L. Sayers, in her masterpiece of detective fiction, *The Nine Tailors,* has the following conversation between an old woman and her pastor.

" 'We mustn't question the ways of Providence,' said the Rector.

" 'Providence?' said the old woman. 'Don't yew talk to me about Providence, I've had enough o' Providence. First he took my husband, and then he took my 'taters, but there's One above as'll teach him to mend his manners, if he don't look out.'

"The Rector was too much distressed to challenge this remarkable piece of theology.

" 'We can but trust in God, Mrs. Giddings,' he said. . . .' "

But whose theology was most confused, the old woman's, or the Rector's? She was at least tackling the problem, but her pastor was avoiding it with a pious phrase.[4]

A lot of people piously avoid the question. "God moves in mysterious ways," they say. But that's not from the Bible. It is misquoted from the English poet William Cowper. The correct quotation in full is, "God moves in a mysterious way, His *wonders* to perform."[5]

The meaning of "providence" has been distorted to make it mean "whatever happens to me," good or bad. "Providence" originally referred to God as a *Provider*. We would not call a human father a good provider if his "providence" consisted in providing poison for his children instead of good food, or leaving them without clothes or shelter. But, as Dorothy Sayers's old lady clearly saw, God is far better than that kind of "providence." He doesn't arbitrarily "take" people's potatoes, or their husbands, for that matter.

How often you hear folk say when someone dies, "God took him," yet the Bible makes it very clear that death didn't and doesn't come from God. It came into the world through sin, and it is always an enemy. "For he must reign, till he hath put all enemies under his feet. The last enemy that shall be destroyed is death," says the Apostle Paul in 1 Corinthians 15:26. God takes His children *out of* death into His kingdom, but death is not a friend or a co-worker of His.

What Would Jesus Do?

It's true that God says through the prophet Isaiah that His thoughts are not our thoughts, nor His ways our ways,[6] but He goes on to say that His ways are heavenly and high above ours; they are not ways of unreasonable cruelty. Since Jesus came, and with the Father gives the Holy Spirit to those who ask, we can have the mind of Christ. His thoughts *can* be our thoughts. We can think the thoughts of God.[7] The Scripture tells how God is showing more and more clearly what He is like, and what He is doing. Jesus perfectly reveals His Father. He says, "If you want to know what God the Father is like, look at Me."[8] If you want to know what God would do in any situation, ask, "What would Jesus do?"

We told in the book *The Holy Spirit and You* how I was asked to pray for a woman who was, the doctors said, going to die very soon. She lived quite far away, but I was to be in her neighborhood, and friends asked me to stop by and see her. Her face was sallow and emaciated from her illness, but she was smiling brightly. She said, "I am reconciled to the fact that my condition is God's will."

How could I argue? She was submitting to God. Isn't that what a Christian is supposed to do? Well, yes, but it might be well to find out what God wants, first, before we assume that the circumstances we face are from Him, and that therefore we should accept them. Is everything that happens God's will? That's what Muslims believe. They accept everything as the will of Allah; in fact, "Islam" means "submission to the will of God." The Muslim does not pray to alter circumstances, but to accept them, whatever they are. Yet this lady, or at least her friends, had asked that I pray for her to be healed. Apparently they did not believe that everything was happening the way God wanted. Yet the woman herself told me she had decided that it was.

I thought a moment and said to her, "If Jesus Himself were to walk into this room what would He do?"

She hesitated briefly, then replied, "Why, He'd heal me!"

"Exactly," I said. "You don't have any doubt of that, do you?"

"No," she answered.

I said, "Well, Jesus said that He only did the things He saw His Father do—that He did nothing of Himself. He also said that He and His Father were so close, as to be like One—that if we had seen Him, we had seen His Father.[9] How can you tell me that Jesus would heal you, but the Father wills that you die of this disease?" Her face brightened even more, "I see what you mean!" she said happily, and then I could pray for her.[10]

You see, God is really and truly good, not indirectly and mysteriously, but in a way we can understand. First John 4:16 says, "God is love, and he that dwelleth in love dwelleth in God, and God in him." He truly desires to do good for the people He has made, if they will allow Him to. If they will not—well, I think it was old Jeremy Taylor who said, "He threatens terrible things if we will not be happy!" God knows that in order to be happy we must come to Him; that there is nothing but misery in store if we run away from Him out into the dark. So, "If a man will not turn, He will whet His sword; He hath bent His bow, and made it ready,"[11] but this is in order to drive people to Him, not away from Him. When my children were little, we lived for a while in a corner house, on two busy streets. We told the kids not to play in the street, but one of them kept on doing it. So I got a little switch and next time this child ran into the street I switched his legs. Was that because I hated him? No, of course not, it was because I loved him, and didn't want him hurt.

Where then does evil come from? Is God *not* all-powerful? Can't He stop malicious and senseless bad things from happening?

God Is Sovereign

God is all-powerful, make no mistake about that. He is "sovereign"—which is just another way of saying He's King. He can create and destroy as He pleases. And God is really good. He created a good world—Genesis says He saw everything He had made, and it was very good.[12] All the way through, the Bible makes it clear that God is a good God, who wants us to be healthy and joyful.

God made the world with everything just as He wanted it, but in order for the world to remain that way, God would have had to continue to keep everything completely under His control. He couldn't have let anything in creation do just as it pleased, because it might upset things.

This is not hard to understand. If you are single, you pretty much control how you live. You can get up when you please and go to bed when you please, eat what you please, vacation where you please, look at what you please on TV, and so forth.

If you marry, however, you give up a good deal of your freedom. There are now two of you who must agree on food, furnishings, schedules, and the like. Your world can no longer be exactly as you want it. And if you have children, things get even more complex. You give up a lot of your liberty, if you allow others into your life. Why do it, then? Because you want to be loved and to have companionship, and are willing to give up much of your freedom in order to have those things.

Well, then, marry a spouse who will do everything you want him or her to do, and bring up your kids the same way! Why not? Because there can't be love if there's no freedom. You wouldn't be likely to marry someone who would do everything you told him or her to, who had no mind of his or her own. If that's what you wanted, you would hire a servant. Indeed the time is coming when you will be able to buy a robot humanoid that will do things just as you want them done, but a robot wouldn't make much of a friend, let alone wife or husband!

A human servant can only be your friend in so far as you decide to treat him as one, and leave him free to do what he wants to do. He can't be your friend if he's simply doing what you tell him because you are paying him, or because he is afraid of you. In the military, close friendship is discouraged between commissioned officers and enlisted men, and in business an employer will hesitate to be too friendly with his employees, because if someone is your friend, you don't like to give him orders.

Of course, a friend may do what you want because he or she loves you and wants to please you, but he's still doing it freely, because he wants to, not because you are requiring it of him in order for him to be your friend. Jesus said to His followers, "You are my friends if you do whatever I tell you,"[13] but Jesus is the only Man who could have said something like that. Only God can make that kind of claim on His friends.

God Limits Himself

Here, then, is the key. If someone is going to love me, he or she's got to be free to choose to hate me. A man can't compel a girl to fall in love with him. If he could get her to behave lovingly toward him by the use of some chemical, or by hypnotism, or by conditioning her in some other way, it wouldn't be love. A little robot may be very "faithful" to its master, like R2D2 in "Star Wars," but that's only because it is programmed to act that way. People are not robots, and programmed "love" is not love at all.

C. S. Lewis said:

A world of automata—of creatures that worked like machines—would hardly be worth creating. The happiness which God designs for His higher creatures is the happiness of being freely, voluntarily united to Him and to each other in an ecstasy of love and light compared with which the most rapturous love between a man and a woman on this earth is mere milk and water. And for that they must be free.[14]

So the all-powerful God created other beings that have free will, in order to expand the possibility for love. But by so doing He created the possibility that these beings would choose what is exactly opposite to what God wants; they would choose to be evil and destructive.

Lewis further says:

If a thing is free to be good it is also free to be bad. And free will is what has made evil possible. Why, then, did God give . . . free will? Because free will, though it makes evil possible, is also the only thing that makes possible any love or goodness or joy worth having.[15]

Love is more important to God than a perfect world. God is willing to take a chance on disorder and rebellion and even pain and death in the creation, if only there can be love. "God does not control. No, much more wonderfully, God loves. Love does not control; rather, it redeems and creates within the pain and joy of a world with freedom . . ."[16]

In his *History of Christianity,* Kenneth Scott Latourette puts it this way:

It is at least an arguable explanation of the seeming contrast that as the gospel is longer in the world and makes its way more widely across the earth, God entrusts men with more knowledge and more mastery of their environment. He does this fully aware of the risk that He is taking, realizing that some will pervert His gifts, but also confident that others will be so gripped by the gospel that they will be stirred and empowered not only to counteract the evil but also to produce fruits far greater than if the possibilities for the abuse of God's gifts had not been present. It is conceivable that this is God's way of dealing with men, that He is seeking to produce men of character, not automatons, and that this can be done only by giving men freedom of choice either to their infinite hurt or to their infinite good, but that He is also sovereign and will not permit evil to get completely out of hand, but will overrule it for His own purposes of love.[17]

By giving us free will God didn't lose any of His power, but He limited the use of His power for a time. Let's say you drive a car provided by your employer. You're on call twenty-four hours a day, and so must always have somewhere to park. Your employer assigns a place in the firm's parking lot just for you. No one else is to use it at any time, not even himself.

Your boss hasn't given up any of his "sovereignty." The car you are driving belongs to him. He could stop you from using it if he wished. He could fire you if he wished. The whole parking lot belongs to him. He could sell it, have it plowed up, or build a building on it, but as long as he has guaranteed you exclusive use of that parking place, he can't park his own car there without contradicting his own orders. He has limited his own freedom.

God's relationship to the world is something like that. He could tear the whole place up if He wanted to—but as long as He decides to work with it, and to leave us free to obey Him or not, He can't keep everything exactly the way He wants it and everything will *not* take place according to His will. To say God can allow you freely to do what you want, while at the same time compelling you to do what *He* wants, is simply double talk.

So everything that happens on this earth isn't caused by God, nor does He necessarily want it to happen. God can't prevent His creatures from doing bad things, and at the same time give them the freedom necessary for them to choose to love Him and each other.

It's misleading, too, to talk of God's "permissive *will.*" People behave wrongly, and accidents and other bad things happen, not necessarily because God wants or wills them to, but because He cannot prevent them without taking away freedom. He permits them because even He, God, has no alternative.

I told how I had to punish my child to keep him from running out into the street. There came a time, though, when I had to let him run where he wanted to. Hopefully by that time he had learned to take care of himself. The only alternative would have been to keep him under lock and key—or tied to the apron strings indefinitely. After I have set him free, if my child gets into trouble or gets hurt, is that because I wanted him to? Of course not. Have I *allowed* him to get hurt? Yes.

The evil in the world, then, doesn't come from God. It comes from wrong and rebellious decisions made by the free beings He has created.

Notes

1. Romans 8:28.
2. Romans 3:7, 8 Jerusalem, AP.
3. Psalms 112:6, 7, RSV.
4. Dorothy L. Sayers, "The Nine Tailors" (New York: Harcourt, Brace & World, Inc., 1962), p. 68. We use the rector's remark as an example of a pious phrase, but that doesn't mean he is an unattractive character in the story. Quite the contrary, he is very much the hero of the piece!
5. William Cowper, "Light Shining out of Darkness," 1774. Hymn No. 310 in the *Hymnal* 1940 of the Episcopal Church, and in many other hymnals. Italics mine.
6. Isaiah 55:8.
7. 1 Corinthians 2:16.
8. John 14:9, AP.
9. John 8:28, 10:30, 14:9.
10. Bennett, *The Holy Spirit and You,* pp. 114, 115.

11. Psalms 7:12 Coverdale, BCP 1928, pronouns referring to God have been capitalized for clarity.

12. Genesis 1:31, et al.

13. John 15:14, AP.

14. Lewis, *Mere Christianity,* p. 52.

15. Loc. cit.

16. The Reverend William G. Burrill, "The Creator's Love," *The Living Church,* Oct. 5, 1980.

17. Latourette, *A History of Christianity* Vol. II, pp. 968–9.

3

Heavenly Warfare

You are an amphibian, able to live in two different elements. Your body is built for living on the earth; but you have a spirit that is made in the image of God, so you're able to relate to the spiritual world. Your spirit is like God, so you are able to respond to Him, and to other people, in love, if you choose to. Your soul, your psychological nature, shares in both worlds.[1]

God put us human beings in charge of planet Earth. "Have dominion over the fish of the sea," said God, "and over the birds of the air and over every living thing that moves upon the earth."[2] "Dominion" means lordship or kingship. The Psalmist says, speaking of mankind, "You have made him little less than a god, you have crowned him with glory and splendour, made him lord over the work of your hands, set all things under his feet."[3]

Unfortunately, the first humans used their freedom to reject God. The Scripture says they were talked into it by one of the powerful *archons,* the spiritual beings God had made to share with Him in creating and maintaining the universe.[4] This *archon* had turned against God, ages before, and ever since had been making trouble, spoiling and destroying wherever he could. In the Bible he is called Satan, which means an enemy, opponent, accuser; or "the devil," which in the Greek means "someone who throws things"—a slanderer.

He convinced the first humans that God was trying to keep them under His thumb, and urged them to disobey God and manage their own lives. He said, "You know, you could be like gods yourselves! You could make up your own minds about what's right and wrong."[5]

They fell for Satan's line, broke fellowship with God, and cut themselves off from His care. They had thought they would then be free agents, but instead they came under Satan's control. He took over the earth spiritually and let loose a flood of other rebel spirits into it, those whom Paul later calls "the rulers of the darkness of this world."[6] The local spiritual world surrounding the earth became filled with these beings, so that God's messengers sometimes had to fight their way through, and even send for reinforcements, as Gabriel did when he came to Daniel.[7] These beings are what Paul is referring to when he speaks of "spiritual powers of evil in the heavens."[8]

Satan and the other rebel spirits tried to get human beings to worship them. In the Old Testament, they turn up under the names of Moloch, Dagon, the Ba'alim, and so forth. In other countries they were called Zeus, Mars, Venus, Thor, Loki, and the rest of the gods and goddesses of pagan mythology. They are still around. In parts of the world where the old religions are still alive, these beings are still worshiped and manifest themselves under the old names. In modern America they are sometimes worshiped, too, but they are more often found as the "spirit guides" of mediums, or creating various kinds of psychic and occult phenomena, and so forth. (One of the reasons astrology is dangerous is that it recognizes these beings as having power when it claims that Mars, Venus, Jupiter, etc., can influence people's lives.)

When Jesus began His ministry, Satan was still ruling the earth. When he tempted Jesus, he "showed him in a flash all the kingdoms of the world. 'All this dominion will I give to you,' he said, 'and the glory that goes with it; for *it has been put in my hands and I can give it to anyone I choose.*"[9] The devil is a liar, but this time he was telling the truth. You notice that Jesus didn't challenge him on it? Three times in the Gospel of John, Jesus refers to Satan as the "ruler [*archon*] of this world."[10]

The Big Change-over

The earth has two branches of living things, vegetable and animal. You'd better be glad it does! You wouldn't do too well if you had to live on water, earth, carbon dioxide, and sunshine! Green plants do that, as you know, by the miracle of photosynthesis; and animals and humans were supposed to feed on those "green things of the earth."[11] It looks, though, as if God did not mean even the plants to be destroyed in order to provide food. It was the fruit and seeds of the plants that were to be eaten, or the foliage, which would grow again. I don't have to cut down my cherry tree to eat its cherries (if the birds don't get them first!) and in the spring and summer we pick leaves of lettuce, but do not destroy the plant.

When human beings gave up their authority to the enemy, though, earth went wild. Spiritually separated from God, and dominated by Satan, destruction became the pattern, not only with humans, but with nature itself. Man had been given authority and power over the animal world, but now animals began to prey on man, and God had to permit men to hunt and kill animals in order to protect themselves, and for food. Genesis 9:1–5 tells the sad tale. Man continued to have power over the animals, but whereas at first he was to rule by love, as God's representative, now he ruled by force and fear.[12]

When He created the world, God established what we call "laws of nature." These weren't really fixed and unchangeable, but stable patterns, so that things would happen predictably. It would be difficult if you weren't sure, for example, that rivers would run downhill, not up, and that water would boil when you heated it, not when you cooled it! The first humans were probably not limited by these "laws," but after they separated from God, and lost control of nature, they became subject to them. Things began to happen by blind cause and effect, what the philosophers call "determinism": what happens today is the end result of a chain of things that have happened in the past. On those occasions when God broke into the chain it was called a "miracle."

What the Original "Program" Was Like

One of the reasons people give for not believing in God is that children are sometimes born with defects and deformities. If there were a loving and all-powerful God He would not allow it, they say.

But there is a God, and He doesn't want children to have defects. Of course not! Can you imagine Jesus creating a defective child? Deformities are often the result of damage to genetic coding. It seems likely that both aging and death, as well as hereditary defects, are the result of accumulating errors in the "program" set up in the genetic material.

God devised the marvelous process of heredity in which all the physical, and perhaps a lot of the mental characteristics are carried in the germ plasm. At the time of fertilization and mitosis, the genes from male and female are freely mixed in various ways. Thus there is an unending variety of different kinds of individuals. God delights in variety. He doesn't want a world of clones!

When the world lost spiritual contact with God, the genetic code continued on as part of the chain of cause and effect, passing along from generation to generation. While human beings were in direct contact with God, anything that went wrong in the course of this procedure would have been immediately corrected. God did not plan defects, or sickness, or aging and death—none of them were in *His* program. But when the contact was lost, there was no longer any way for accidents or damage to the germ plasm to be corrected. This is why some children come into the world with defective bodies. Even those who are tolerably complete at the outset are still subject to aging, which means that as time goes by, the code gets more and more distorted from its original schedule, and the various parts of the body are rebuilt less and less according to the original pattern.

God's Way Is Love, Not Force

Of course, when human beings turned against Him and let the enemy take over, God could have wiped out the whole mess, Satan and all. Or He could have cancelled free will and made everything just as He wanted it again. Right from the days of the Greek city-states, it was recognized that if a free society began to misuse its liberty and become disordered, one way to cure the problem was for a tyrant to take over and straighten things out. Today we would call this a dictatorship. First, though, the dictator or tyrant must take away freedom, usually by establishing martial law, then he or she can force things into order. I am old enough to remember how people applauded Adolf Hitler when he first came into power because he made the trains run on time in Germany. Soon labor/management disputes, social disorder, everything was quickly brought into line—but at what a cost to the German people, to Hitler's victims, and to the world!

When freedom is taken away, human dignity is lost; the possibility of cooperating and obeying for love's sake is lost, and darkness follows quickly, as it did in Nazi Germany, and does today in those nations that are under communism. (There are "social planners" in the free world, too, who teach that the solution to man's problems can only be found by his giving up his freedom and his dignity and putting himself into the hands of "conditioners." Read B. F. Skinner, *Beyond Freedom and Dignity,* and C. S. Lewis, *The Abolition of Man.*)

God refused to move in as a dictator. He would rather let the world suffer from disorder and leave people still free to respond to Him voluntarily. God is not a tyrant, and He doesn't want slaves. He wants people to acknowledge Him as King because they love Him, so He kept on honoring freedom of choice and permitted Satan to continue his control over the earth, while God set about the long job of redeeming the world, not by force, but by love.

This situation will not continue forever, for God "has appointed a day, in which he will judge the world in righteousness. . . ."[13] "The Lord is King," says the Psalmist, "be the people never so impatient;

he sitteth between the Cherubim, be the earth never so unquiet."[14] The rebellion in the world does not touch God's kingship. He could silence the rebels with a word, but He waits patiently to work matters out on Earth, giving people a chance to decide whether they want Him or not. "God is a righteous Judge, strong, and patient; and God is provoked every day."[15] When everybody has chosen, God will use His power to clear all evil and malice completely out of His creation, leaving nothing but love and beauty and joy.

God Didn't Stop Loving

God did not stop loving the human race; human beings stopped loving and trusting Him. In Jesus' story of the prodigal son, which He surely meant to be a picture of the way God deals with His children, the father never stopped loving the young man. He watched and waited, and when his son finally made the decision to come home, he ran to meet him, and gave him a big party. He freely and fully forgave him, because he knew his attitude had entirely changed. He had "come to himself."

God's Rescue Project

The story of God's rescue project for the world really begins when He got one man's attention. The man's name was Abram, later renamed Abraham. God promised Abraham that He would not only bless him, but his family too, and that through his descendants the whole world was going to be blessed. In carrying out His promise, God took some of Abraham's grandchildren, the children of Jacob (Israel), and separated them from the rest of humanity so that He could teach them what He was like, and begin to work through them to rescue the world from the powers of darkness. The tribes around were worshipping fallen *archons* and demonic spirits as gods and goddesses. God didn't want His "chosen people" to get involved with the terrible things these tribes were doing under the influence of these spirits, such as ritual prostitution and human sacrifice—often of children. He set up a "quarantine." His people were to keep to themselves. They were to drive the other tribes out of the country and even kill them if they would not go. This wasn't because God hated the other peoples or wanted to hurt them, but because the hope of the whole human race depended on what He was doing with the Israelites, and nothing could be allowed to interfere with it.

God gave them special rules and regulations. He gave them leaders, like Moses and David, and prophets—men and women who would speak and act for Him. At those times when God used His supernatural power to help His people, He usually acted through these human leaders. It was Moses who called down the plagues on Egypt and opened and closed the Red Sea.[16] It was Elijah who called for the drought in the days of King Ahab, and also brought it to an end.[17]

The chosen people kept on disobeying and rebelling, however, and the whole plan seemed doomed to fail. Finally, most of them were hauled off as prisoners to other countries. There was a "righteous remnant" left, though, and in that little group God was able to accomplish the great Miracle He had been planning, the coming of Jesus into the world.

In the Old Testament, God was revealing Himself, but the picture was incomplete. This is because He could not communicate with them directly. In Jesus He showed exactly what He was like. Jesus said plainly, "He that sees Me, sees the Father!"[18] Now people had a clear opportunity to decide whether they wanted God or not.

People did decide. Some rejected Jesus. Some accepted Him. In John 3:18, 19, Jesus said that no one who believed in Him would be judged, but those who refused to believe were already judged by the very fact they didn't accept Him. "This is the judgment," said Jesus, "that light is come into the world, and men loved darkness rather than light. . . ."[19]

Most of the rulers of the Jewish people (all that was left of the "chosen" descendants of Abraham) decided to reject Jesus. They had Him arrested and tried and condemned as a threat to the public peace. He allowed Himself to be executed by the Roman authorities.

It looked like a total victory for Satan and his forces, who were, of course, behind the whole thing, but it turned out just the other way. By His death Jesus cancelled the guilt that had held mankind tied to Satan. Before this, the "Accuser" could say to God, "These people betrayed You, and now look at the terrible things they are doing to each other and to the world You gave them to take care of. You're a God of fair dealing, and fairness demands that they pay for all that!" But God just said, "I'll pay for it!" God not only didn't stop loving us; He actually sent His beloved Son to die for us and set us free, so that we could come home to Him.

Jesus Has the Power

Jesus didn't stay dead. His physical body rose from death, completely "glorified," that is, controlled by His Spirit. He wasn't limited any more by space and time. He could come and go as He wished.

He told His friends, "All power is given to Me in Heaven and Earth."[20] They thought He would immediately use the power to make himself King, drive out the Romans, and rule the earth from Jerusalem, with them as the top men in His government.[21] But Jesus wasn't going to become a dictator either, nor was He going to make Himself King of a limited human nation.

He told His disciples they were going to help Him establish a larger and more wonderful Kingdom than they dreamed. "Go into the whole world," Jesus told them, "and tell the good news to the whole creation."[22] They were going to help Him set up God's Kingdom over the whole world, and God was going to rule, not by force, but by grace, which means "love in action." "God in Christ was reconciling the world to himself."[23]

Then Jesus breathed the Holy Spirit into them, and gave them the new kind of life He had promised, His kind of life, "eternal" life, which means ageless life, life that doesn't get tired or bored, or wear out. He told them that after the Holy Spirit had "clothed them with power," they would go everywhere telling people about Him and doing the sort of things He had been doing.[24] Jesus had come like a landing party to invade the rebellious earth and begin reclaiming it. Now the people who were filled and empowered by the Spirit became part of the beachhead Jesus had established, and which He wanted spread as far and wide as possible.

This is where you and I come into the story. On the Day of Pentecost, Jesus poured out the same gift of the Holy Spirit "on all flesh." After that, the Spirit of God could come to anyone who would receive Him, and fill that person with His power and love, His gifts and fruit; then he or she could go and spread the good news, and do what Jesus did, just as much as the first disciples.

A Picture of the Kingdom

A country is different from a kingdom. A country is a particular piece of earth, but a kingdom is made up of people who accept someone as king. The *country* of England is a largish island off the shore of Europe, but the *kingdom* of England is some sixty million people who acknowledge Elizabeth II as their monarch. If an enemy conquered the country of England and moved the people to another part of the world, along with the queen, the kingdom of England would no longer be in the country called England, but in the new place where the queen and her people were now living. I firmly believe God has a heavenly country, but God's Kingdom on earth is made up of people. When you accept Jesus, you are accepting God as your king, so you become a part of God's Kingdom. God is not yet ruling as sovereign King of the earthly country; that's why bad things are still happening. But He *is* King in the hearts of His people.

The Apostle Paul says of Jesus that, "He must be King *until* He has put all His enemies under His feet," and that after He has "done away with every sovereignty, authority, and power" He will hand the kingship over to his Father, "that God may be all in all."[25]

But if the Kingdom of God has not yet come on the Earth, if Jesus hasn't yet "put all His enemies under His feet" and "done away with every sovereignty, authority, and power"; if these things are still dominating the earth and causing war, hate, crime, and sickness, in what sense is Jesus a King now? Where is He reigning? The answer is obvious. While earth is still in the process of being brought back under Jesus' rule, He is ruling in those who have received Him as King. Because of man's free will, God is not sovereignly ruling the earth as yet, but He is expressing His sovereignty, His kingship, through His people. Matthew 10:8 says that Jesus told His disciples to "heal the sick . . . raise the dead, cast out evil spirits." The orders have never been changed. We have power to chase out the enemy, and to say and do the kind of things Jesus did and said. In fact, Jesus said we would do greater things than He did.[26] People are going to see Jesus working through us, just as they did with the disciples in New Testament times. That is the way God's sovereignty is going to be expressed on earth until Jesus' victory is complete.

Most Christians believe that after we have done everything we can to bring the world back to God, Jesus Himself will come in Person to finish the job. After everyone who wants to come to God has had a chance to do so, He will use whatever power is necessary to get the earth completely straightened out, and like Heaven.

Israel, Old and New

The Israelites in the old days were told the Promised Land was theirs and that they had power to chase the Canaanites out of it,[27] and God promised to bless the whole world through them.[28] But they did a half-hearted job of driving out the Canaanites, with the result that the Canaanites tormented and corrupted them. Moreover, they didn't grasp the vision that they were to bless the whole world; instead, they drew back into a narrow nationalism, thinking God was only interested in *them.*

In the same way, we Christians have not used God's sovereign power in us to drive out Satan, but have let him continue to corrupt and harm us. More than that, we have actually blamed God for many of the bad things Satan has been doing. In fact, most Christians still don't take the devil seriously and many don't even believe he exists. They think he's just a comic opera character, with red tights and pitchfork!

Then, too, just as the chosen people did in the old days, Christians behave as if they were God's pet lambs, as if He didn't care about the rest of the world. Many have what I call a "rapture complex." They feel the world is past saving anyway, and that all they need to do is say their prayers, read the Bible, and stay out of trouble until the Lord comes to take them out of it all! They do not believe the power of the Holy Spirit is available to them, yet they know that without it they are no match for Satan, and so for their own spiritual safety they must be taken away before the going gets too rough.[29]

There's Work to Be Done!

Jesus told us to pray "Thy Kingdom *come* on earth as it is in Heaven," and He would not have said that if it had already come. There's no sorrow, sickness, pain or death in Heaven, and that's hardly true of this world we live in! Revelation says, speaking of Jesus' final victory, "The kingdoms of this world are become the kingdoms of our Lord, and of his Christ."[30] Why would they have to "become" His kingdoms if they already *were?* Reading the daily paper, can you really believe that Jesus is ruling the kingdoms of this world now? Isn't it only too clear that Satan is still in charge?

But Jesus defeated him? Yes, Jesus now has the power to utterly conquer the devil and all his works, but He won't use it directly. He has given the power to us and unless we use it the powers of darkness are still going to be running things.

You Can't Fight City Hall

If you think God is already functioning as absolute King and Ruler of this world, you are likely to accept bad things without any resistance, believing them to be the will of God, planned or permitted by God. If God's doing it, how can you fight "City Hall"? All you can do is put up with it, and after you have shown patient endurance, maybe God will pull off the heat and tell you you've passed the test! If you think this way and function this way, God will not be able to work through you to change things. You will be passive, God's Kingdom will be indefinitely delayed, and Satan will continue to dominate the earth.

Do you think your life on this planet is a kind of practice maneuver? Not so. The obstacles in your life aren't set up by God to test your faith and courage. So many people, when something goes wrong in their lives, will say, "I wonder why God's doing this to me?" I've even heard it taught that God and Satan are working together sort of as a team to test us! That's not true. Satan is a real enemy, and there is a real war on. If there weren't a war, why would the Scriptures warn us to "put on the whole armor of God"?[31] We grow strong by having to fight the bad things in this world, that's true, but the bad stuff comes from Satan, not from God. God is on our side. Paul asks, "If God be for us, who can be against us?"[32] It would be difficult for soldiers to fight wholeheartedly if they had to wonder whether their commander was cooperating with the enemy to make things hard for them.

God doesn't cause the evils done to His children and to His world; He's trying to get them corrected. Jesus did not tolerate sickness or death when it crossed His path. Wherever He went, He changed events to match the will of His Father. Ask yourself in which direction He changed things. A friend of mine says, "Jesus never knocked people down, He always lifted them up." Jesus didn't want to make people sad; He said He came to bring life and joy.[33] He didn't make them sick, He made them well; and whenever we hear of Him encountering people who had died, He raised them back to life. We are commissioned to do the same sort of things, but we will not have the faith and confidence to do them if we have even a tiny notion that the evil things may be the will of God, or are caused or allowed by God.

Victory Over Mountains

Here in the State of Washington, when Mount St. Helens erupted violently on May 18, 1980, some folks were quick to say that it was God's doing, His vengeance. Posters came out showing the mountain erupting, with the caption underneath: "NOW THAT I HAVE YOUR ATTENTION!!" I said to the people at church on Sunday morning after the third major eruption, "Jesus says by faith we can move mountains.[34] Let's command Mount St. Helens to quiet down. Let's take authority over that mountain!" We agreed on that. I don't know how many others were praying that way too, but I do know that since that terrible May 18th eruption, although there have certainly been further incidents, the mountain has not caused the continuing destruction that was feared. I hope people will continue to pray for the mountain to be kept under control, and not accept its violence as a sign of the apocalyptic vengeance of God.

When St. Helens erupted, a number of people near the mountain lost their lives and property. Were they sinners more than others? The ash went eastward, and blanketed many areas, creating serious problems. We didn't get any in Seattle to speak of. Did that mean Seattle is more righteous than Yakima or Wenatchee? Jesus dealt with this when He said, "Those eighteen men who were killed when that tower collapsed in Siloam, were they greater sinners than the rest of the people in Jerusalem? I tell you they weren't, but unless you change your attitude, you're all going to perish."[35]

We'd better be very careful how we label natural catastrophes "acts of God"—they may be actions of the enemy. Satan is, after all, "the prince of the power of the air."[36] There are plenty of examples scattered through history of people rebuking storms and turning aside tornadoes by the power of the Spirit. They certainly weren't fighting against God.

Scientists have been predicting a violent earthquake in California, and some people have been rather smacking their lips over the terrible punishment that is coming to the "wicked" folk out there! I appreciate my old friend, the late Agnes Sanford, who told in her book, *Sealed Orders,* how she moved to California and intentionally purchased a home near the famous San Andreas fault. There she said she could pray for the troubled earth, so there would *not* be a destructive earthquake![37] God is not trying to get people killed, but to keep them alive so they will have the chance to accept Him.

God doesn't only want to work through us to heal the sick, and cast out evil spirits, but also to change adverse circumstances to bring His world into right order. And that includes volcanoes!

I'm not saying God could not or would not cause physical catastrophes, nor am I saying that He has not or will not do so. One of these days, says God, He's going to shake the earth and bring down "every high thing."[38] But those are supernatural interventions, not natural happenings, and when God does this kind of thing, He lets it be known.

Dealing with Three Areas: The Environment

There are three areas in which God wants us to take authority: The first is our physical environment. We mentioned people commanding storms to turn aside. It's been said that "everybody talks about the weather, but no one does anything about it."[39] For Christians, that should be a "called bluff"! It was George Müller, as I recall, who was traveling on the Great Lakes to an important engagement when the ship was halted by a dense fog. The captain shook his head, saying they were not able to proceed till the fog lifted. Müller asked the captain to come with him into the cabin and pray. They did so. Then Müller said, "Captain, if you will come outside you will find the fog has gone," and it had.

I have myself seen undoubted answers to this kind of prayer, and not necessarily because of a serious emergency. Several years ago Rita and I went down to spend the Labor Day weekend with our younger son and his family in Longview, Washington. Saturday was bright, clear, and warm, but Sunday the weather collapsed, and by Monday, the day we had planned to go to the beach, it was pouring rain, thundering, lightning, just about everything that our Northwest weather can do! Nevertheless we set out for the beach, hoping that perhaps it might clear up later, although it didn't look like it. As we were going along through rain and storm, I said, "Let's pray for sunshine at Cannon Beach."

So we agreed on that. It rained all the way until we approached our destination, and then began to clear up. When we got to the beach, the clouds had been blown back and were lying around the horizon. The sand had been soaked four inches deep by the rain, but we had warm sunshine all day, and the place virtually to ourselves.

People say, "What if you're praying for sunshine, and someone else is praying for rain?" Well, that's easy! It'll rain for them, and the sun will shine on you! Why not?

I believe we can take authority over volcanoes, earthquakes, storms. I believe we could often be protected against other physical catastrophes if we were only more sensitive to God's voice. A friend was driving over the Cascade Mountains. He was on the inside lane of the highway, next to the oncoming traffic. Suddenly, he reports, an inner voice said, "Pull to the right!" He did so, just in time to avoid being hit by a huge truck that came over the crest of the hill on the wrong side of the center line.

I know that I don't listen to God nearly enough, and yet I'm tempted to blame Him if I get in a mess!

Authority over the physical environment includes authority over things which affect health. A lot of sickness comes about because the world is out of control. God did not plan for bacteria to prey on us, any more than He planned for the higher animals to prey on us, or us on them. There is a good deal of evidence that when people are truly moving in the power of the Holy Spirit, they have supernatural defense against sickness. "They that wait upon the Lord shall renew their strength."[40]

Nothing in Scripture says God sends sickness to His faithful people—but I'm going to deal with that subject later in the book.

Authority Over Carelessness or Malice of Others

The second area where we can take authority is over the carelessness and malice of other people, which is where most of our troubles come from. And here again we have, I think, more strength than we use, judging from Jesus' example. Jesus could not force people to change their minds or attitudes, but He did not allow them to harm Him without His permission. Just before He was crucified He told the disciples He could call twelve legions (72,000) angels to help

Him, if He chose.[41] His death was something He permitted to happen; He was not taken to the cross against His will. When they came to arrest Him, John records, Jesus released just a tiny bit of His power, and they were all thrown backwards onto the ground.[42] He said, "I lay down My life, no man takes it from Me!"[43]

Attempts had been made to destroy Him long before this. In Nazareth His fellow townsmen tried to kill Him, but He simply "passed through their midst."[44] John 8:59 tells how, when the Pharisees were about to stone Him, He "hid Himself, and went out of the temple, going through the midst of them, and so passed by." In both cases this must have been a supernatural "hiding." Jesus confused them in much the same way, perhaps, as God confused the people of Sodom in Genesis 19:11.

On the island of Paphos, when Elymas the sorcerer interfered with Paul while he was telling the Roman deputy, Sergius Paulus, about Jesus, Paul used the power of the Spirit to blind Elymas temporarily.[45] Everyone knows how Peter dealt with Ananias and Sapphira.[46] It's true these supernatural deliverances—such as Daniel in the lion's den, Peter being released from prison, the breaking of the dungeon for Paul and Silas at Philippi—seem to come at the will of the Holy Spirit, yet perhaps He is more willing than we assume. There is an interesting passage in Hebrews telling of those "who through faith subdued kingdoms, wrought righteousness, obtained promises, stopped the mouths of lions, quenched the violence of fire, escaped the edge of the sword, out of weakness were made strong, waxed valiant in fight, turned to flight the armies of the aliens. Women received their dead raised to life again"; then it goes on, "and others were tortured, *not accepting deliverance, that they might obtain a better resurrection.*"[47]

Do we often put up with things that happen to us that we aren't supposed to and don't need to put up with, because we too quickly decide that God does not want us to "accept deliverance"?

Nearly twenty years ago, one of the bishops of my own denomination was deeply interested in the renewal of the work of the Holy Spirit. He was making arrangements for me to come before the House of Bishops to tell about my experience, and had collected a large number of written testimonies from people who had received the freedom of the Holy Spirit. Before he could carry out his plans, he died. His death was a tremendous loss to us all. I believe that renewal in the Episcopal church was set back by ten years and more. Was this God's will? Would this man have been healed, if the people of God had been more aware of the need to resist the enemy, had acted in faith that God did not want him to die?

Where War Comes From

God is often blamed for international war, which makes no sense at all. The careless and malicious choices of human beings are the reason for war, too. James the Apostle says: "Where do these wars and battles between yourselves first start? Isn't it precisely in the desires fighting inside your own selves? You want something and you haven't got it; so you are prepared to kill."[48]

God Always Has a Better Plan

When you fail to get a prayer answered when you were sure that what you were asking was what God wanted, you will find that somewhere in the situation a human being got in the way, and by his or her free choice interfered with what God was trying to do.

We'll say you have a good job, but you're offered a better one in another city. You and your wife believe in checking with the Lord, and when you do, you both feel sure He wants you to move to the new city and the new job. You get Scriptures that talk clearly to you about stepping out in faith. All the doors fly open. You find a buyer for your house at a price you feel is fair. You find exactly the house you need in the new community, available to you at just the right time. The new job seems ideal. You give notice at your old job, and all plans are in order. It's obvious God is leading you.

Then comes the blow. The new job falls through. Someone up the corporate ladder pulls strings to get someone else into the position that had been promised to you. What a mess! Everything is in confusion. Another person has already been hired to take your place in your old job, and what will you do about your house, and about the one you have arranged to buy in the other town?

What happened? Did God "build you up for a big letdown"? That wouldn't really be much of a way for God to behave, would it, if He wanted people to trust Him? The confusion and disappointment was not caused by God, but by the man who pulled strings to get someone else that job instead of you. God will not force His will on people. They can interfere with and delay God's plans—temporarily.

If something like this happens to you, and you think God has let you down, you'll either be angry with God and decide not to trust Him next time, or you'll passively accept it as one of God's "mysterious ways." But if you realize it isn't God's fault, and continue to trust Him, you'll hear Him say something like, "Oh, I'm sorry about that. That man interfered at the last minute. But don't worry! I've got a better plan." He'll gather all the pieces together and you'll end up with a better job than the one you'd expected. If "Plan A" fails, due to the carelessness, greed, or malice of humankind, God always has Plan B, and then, if necessary, Plan C. Keep on trusting Him, and get away from the notion that He is frivolous and erratic, and that you can never know what He's going to do to you. God may not always allow you to use the miraculous power of the Holy Spirit to protect yourself against the malice of other human beings, as Paul did with Elymas the sorcerer, but He won't let you down. He'll just give you the wisdom to go another route.

One well-known Christian writer says that God sometimes steps aside and lets Satan in, which reminds me of the wry story of the father who was trying to teach his little boy about life. He put the youngster up on the piano, and then held out his arms and said, "Jump, son, daddy'll catch you." When the youngster jumped, the father stepped aside. As the boy picked himself up from the floor, the father said, "First lesson, sonny, don't never trust *nobody,* not even your father!" That's certainly not what God's trying to teach us! If God were like that, there would be no point in trying to follow His leading; the only thing to do would be to make our own way, hoping that He would sometimes choose to help. But of course God is not like that. He wants us to learn to fight the enemy, to endure and continue to trust Him when things are rough, but He isn't going to play tricks on us.

Resist the Devil

The third area in which we can take authority is over things which are the direct work of the devil. We are left in no doubt at all how we are to deal with *him*. We are to resist him, and he will run away![49] Jesus said, "Behold, I give unto you power to tread on serpents and scorpions, and over all the power of the enemy, and nothing shall by any means hurt you."[50] Don't forget that the main fight is not against people, but against these spiritual beings, who are, directly or indirectly, the source of all our troubles.[51]

Any time you suspect that the enemy or one of his henchmen has a direct hand in circumstances, never hesitate to order him or them off the property in the Name of Jesus. They have to go.

In Conclusion

Let's stop playing into the enemy's hands by passively accepting everything that happens as God's will. Let's stop turning people away from God by picturing Him as an unloving tyrant.

When Paul says God, "works all things after the counsel of His own will,"[52] he is saying God has a predetermined goal in mind, and is working toward it. He's going to get there "in the fullness of time." He's looking to us to let Him work in us and through us to help bring about that day.

It's great to know that the team is going to win, but the victory can be postponed if the players don't listen to the coach, and if each tries to play the game in his own way.

Moving Right Along

As you move right along with the Lord, try to keep your balance so you can move effectively and quickly. As you walk in His Spirit,

God's sovereignty functions in and through you. Don't blame your loving Father for destructive and harmful things. Take responsibility for your own sins and errors of judgment, and ask God's pardon where you've been wrong.

There is a war on, so don't lay down your weapons and think there's nothing to be done until Jesus comes back. Don't exaggerate your importance, but do know that God is counting on you to let His strength work through your weakness.

Let Jesus be King. Love Him, honor Him, make Him the center of your life, teach your family about Him. Follow Him, and try to do *what* He says, *when* He says. Speaking for myself, this isn't easy. I forget regularly. Then if things don't go well, I am likely to say, "Why, Lord?" Jesus said He would always be with us,[53] and the writer of Hebrews quotes Him as saying, "I will never leave you nor forsake you."[54] Actually that last verse in Greek reads: "I will never, never leave you, and I will not, not, not forsake you." Isn't that great? So I say to the Lord, "Lord, I've got a lot of great plans for today! You're really going to like them! I even prayed about them a little bit. So come on, Lord, You said You'd never leave me. Please go with me today and help me with my plans."

Along about noon, I may feel like saying, "Lord! You said You'd never fail me nor forsake me, but I'm having a terrible day! Nothing is working out. Everybody I've tried to call on has been out. I've lost a good account, and to make matters worse, my car's got a flat tire! What's the matter?"

And if I'm listening I might hear the Lord say, "My dear boy, I'm right here. I haven't left you at all. I don't like the kind of day we're having either. May I suggest that this afternoon, instead of taking *Me* with *you,* where *you* decide to go, you let *Me* take you with *Me* where *I* decide to go? I think we'd get along better!" He won't leave you, but when you force Him to follow you, instead of you following Him, you get in trouble. But when you remember that He is the leader, isn't it amazing how everything falls into place?

When Jesus said after His victory, "All authority is given to Me in heaven and earth," He immediately said to His followers, *"Go* therefore."[55] It's no accident that God put these two statements together. He's planning and depending on us to go into the world with

His same authority. Through Jesus the power and authority to take this world back from the powers of darkness has been put into our hands.

Let's sing, "All hail, King Jesus," and then live it!

Notes

1. For a detailed teaching on this read *Trinity of Man,* by Dennis and Rita Bennett. See bibliography.
2. Genesis 1:28b KJV Mod.
3. Psalms 8:5 Jerusalem Bible.
4. We usually call them "angels," but this brings up a picture of a lady with wings! "Angel" really means messenger, and refers to only one kind of *archon.* Human messengers are sometimes called "angels," as in Revelation 1–3.
5. Genesis 3 AP.
6. Ephesians 6:12.
7. Daniel 10:13, 20.
8. Ephesians 6:12c literal translation.
9. Luke 4:6 NEB, italics mine.
10. John 12:31; 14:30; 16:11 literal.
11. Genesis 1:29, 30.
12. Genesis 9:2.
13. Acts 17:31 KJV Mod.
14. Psalms 99:1 Coverdale (BCP 1928).
15. Psalms 7:12 Coverdale (BCP 1928).
16. Exodus 7–15.
17. 1 Kings 18.
18. John 14:9 AP.
19. John 3:18, 19 literal Greek.
20. Matthew 28:18 KJV Mod.
21. Acts 1:6–8.
22. Mark 16:15 literal.
23. 2 Corinthians 5:19 Jerusalem Bible.
24. John 14:12; Acts 1:8.
25. 1 Corinthians 15:24–28 Jerusalem Bible. For clarity in quoting, I have rearranged the order of the verses and capitalized personal pronouns pertaining to God.
26. John 14:12.
27. Leviticus 26:6–8.
28. Genesis 12:3; 22:18; 28:14.

29. I don't mean to be passing judgment on any particular theory about the "end times" or the "tribulation." I sometimes wonder though, what the Christians in Communist or Muslim countries, who are being persecuted now for their faith, think of their brothers and sisters in the free world who spend so much of their time speculating about when the "tribulation" is going to begin. I really think they would say: "It's already started, friends!"

30. Revelation 11:15.

31. Ephesians 6:10–18.

32. Romans 8:31.

33. John 10:10; 15:11.

34. Matthew 17:20.

35. Luke 13:4, 5 AP.

36. Ephesians 2:2.

37. Agnes Sanford, *Sealed Orders,* pp. 307–11.

38. Isaiah 2:15, 19, 21; 13:13, et al.

39. I thought this was Mark Twain, but *Bartlett's Familiar Quotations* attributes it to Charles Dudley Warner, in an article in *The Hartford Courant* in 1897.

40. Isaiah 40:31a.

41. Matthew 26:53.

42. John 18:6.

43. John 10:18 AP.

44. Luke, 4:30.

45. Acts 13:6–12.

46. Acts 5:5–11.

47. Hebrews 11:33 italics mine.

48. James 4:1 Jerusalem Bible.

49. James 4:7.

50. Luke 10:19.

51. Ephesians 6:12.

52. Ephesians 1:11b KJV Mod.

53. Matthew 28:20.

54. Hebrews 13:5 KJV Mod.

55. Matthew 28:18, 19.

4

The Value of Praise

In 1960, I came to be pastor of a little Episcopal church in Seattle that was due to be closed after some forty years of struggling to exist. The people were discouraged. I had myself recently experienced a new release in the Holy Spirit, and some of them asked me about it. Soon many of them began to have new freedom, and the church started to revive.[1]

Not long after, someone complained, "At the coffee hour after church, people are saying, 'Praise the Lord!' "

Nuff said! I warned the guilty ones, "Watch it! Don't huddle together at the coffee hour and say 'praise the Lord'! Don't give the impression that you have some kind of exclusive thing going. Get out there among 'em!" They got the point, and I never had another complaint of that kind.

But wasn't it a bit odd? The person complaining had just come from the morning service, where he had taken part in a liturgy the words of which were almost entirely praise to God, yet he objected because some of his friends continued to praise the Lord informally at the coffee hour. Obviously, for him, praise was something you did only in church. The people praising God around the coffee urn must be going "off the deep end," or they had formed a clique, and "praise the Lord" was their password!

It would have bothered me, too, a couple of years before! In those days I'd had a good-sized parish in the Los Angeles area. I knew Jesus as my Savior. I knew what it was to experience God's presence. I believed wholeheartedly in what I was doing as a pastor. I enjoyed teaching. I believed in the offices and sacraments of the Church. I prayed for the sick, and saw people healed from time to time. But if you had come up to me after church on Sunday morning and said, "Praise the Lord!" just like that, I would have been embarrassed.

But after the release or baptism in the Holy Spirit, God became real in a way I could not have imagined, and I began to understand praise.

I would wake up in the morning praising God. I would find myself praising Him at noon, driving down the freeway in the smog. I might get caught up in praise with an informal group of friends in someone's house at 11 P.M. I would fall asleep at night listening to my spirit, moved by the Holy Spirit, saying, "Praise the Lord! Praise the Lord!" inside me. I would kneel at my bedside to pray, and get caught up in praising instead. I would sometimes be praising God in my dreams. There was nothing more exciting and satisfying than praising Him.

It's really quite simple. When you love someone, you want to tell them. If a man loves a woman, he tells her so. He tells her how wonderful she is. He brings her gifts and does nice things for her. This is a liturgy of praise being offered by one human being to another. We praise our wives or husbands, our children, our students, our employees. If there is a writer or a musician whose work has specially inspired you, and you meet him or her personally, you won't spend your time making small talk. You'll pour out your heart in praise to him or her, trying to express just how much his or her songs or books have meant to you.

Praise Is Not the Same As Thanks

Don't confuse praise with thanks. Thanks and praise are very similar, but they are not the same. It's important to say "thank you" to God, and to people. The Scripture says over and over that we should be thankful. But you don't have to know someone personally in order to thank them. This is why you can thank someone you don't know, someone you've never seen.

A short time ago someone called and said a friend of hers had a tape duplicator he wanted to give to be used for Christian work, and were we interested? I said "Yes, we are," and in due time we received the equipment and wrote a letter expressing our sincere thanks to the giver. To this day we have not met him in person, but that didn't stop us from thanking him for his kindness. You can thank someone you've never met.

You thank the woman who holds the door for you at the post office when you have your arms full of packages, or the fellow who lets you into the line of traffic on the freeway.

You can't *praise* these people, though. You couldn't truly say to the girl holding the door, "Oh, you're always so kind. You're such a thoughtful person." You don't know her. All you know is that she's holding the door for you, and for that you can say "thanks." Maybe she never held a door for anyone in her life before, and never will again. Maybe tomorrow she'll slam it in your face! You thank her for her kind action, without needing to know what she is usually like. However, if you met her at the post office every day, and she always held the door for you, you could then say, "You're *always* so helpful! You're so kind!" *That's* a statement about what she *is*, not about what she's doing. You could say it even if she didn't get to hold the door that day. That's praise. You're getting to know her. You have to *know* someone if you're going to praise him or her.

If a man's wife fixes his favorite food for supper, he will thank her (if he's smart!). If they were having supper with friends, he'd say "thank you" to the friend's wife. Or if he's especially enjoyed a meal at a restaurant, he may send thanks to the chef, whom he has never met and perhaps never will meet.

With his wife, though, he can go beyond thanks and say "Honey, you're a great cook!" He knows his wife's cooking and so can *praise* her for it. Even though she's been away at her mother's, and hasn't fixed him a meal for two weeks, he can greet her hopefully when she gets off the plane with "Hi, honey! You're a terrific cook!" He can go far beyond this and say, "You're a wonderful wife!"

When he does this, his wife will probably not preen herself and say "Well, I'm glad you finally recognized how great I am!" No, she will say something like, "Well, you're pretty nice, yourself, you know. You're a wonderful husband!" And this opens the way for love to grow and deepen between them.

With God it's no different. You can *thank* God for things even though you do not yet know Him personally, but to *praise* Him you have to get acquainted with Him, and experience what He is like. Praise is telling God you think He's wonderful, and how much you love and appreciate Him. It isn't flattery, because it is truthful. Flattery is saying things you don't mean in order to earn someone's favor. Praise is just pouring out your true feelings about someone you love.

Praising another human being helps you to *receive* love from him or her. If you have just listened to a fine performance at a concert, you express praise by applauding. This will not only please the artist, but will make him want to perform even better. The applause is itself a part of the process by which the artist is encouraged and enabled to pour out his talents. Not only that, but as you praise his skill, you make yourself more open to enjoy it. In the same way, praising God makes you more open to receive love from Him. It doesn't make Him *begin* to love you—He loved you long before you loved Him; but as you praise Him you are more open to receive His love, and He is able to pour out more love to you.

Heaven is filled with the praises of God, and earth is supposed to be, too. This doesn't mean you shouldn't do anything else, but that you should try to keep praising Him in your heart and with your lips, no matter what you are doing. This way everything you are doing will become a part of praising God. This is what Paul meant when he said we are to "do all to the glory of God."[2]

Why Would We Need to Be Balanced in Praise?

Surely we can't overdo praising God? No, but we can praise Him from wrong motives, or with the wrong idea of why He wants us to praise Him. We can praise Him in ways that will offend other people.

A youngster in Sunday School was told that the way to get prayers answered was to praise the Lord. "Oh," he responded, "I see. You have to sucker Him in!"

It's true that if you praise God, you will get good things from Him. God says He'll bless us if we praise Him. Praise opens the way for prayers to be answered, for healings and miracles to happen. The Psalmist says:

> Let the peoples praise thee, O God; yea, let all the peoples praise thee. Then shall the earth bring forth her increase; and God, even our own God, shall give us his blessing.[3]

God is good, and He wants to do you good. He isn't an angry God who has to be propitiated as the pagan gods were supposed to be. You don't have to mollify Him by saying nice words, flattering Him. You don't have to praise Him in order to persuade Him to do good things for you, or to keep Him from doing bad things to you.

God isn't the problem; I am the problem. God doesn't withhold His blessings, but I often withhold expressing my love to Him. When I praise Him, I become more open to receive from Him, and all kinds of good things can happen. "They who seek the Lord shall want no manner of thing that is good."[4] "They that wait upon the Lord shall renew their strength; they shall mount up with wings as eagles; they shall run, and not be weary; and they shall walk, and not faint."[5] ("Waiting" on the Lord does not mean "waiting around" for the Lord, but giving expectant attention to Him. It is the same as "waiting on" someone at the table: serving them, and watching to see what they want.)

These blessings are spin-offs from praise, though. You don't praise God *in order* to get the blessings. If that were your purpose in praising, it wouldn't be praise. You don't use praise as a gadget to manipulate God. When you praise God, you get your eyes off your needs and the troubles that surround you, and focus on what He *is,* not on what He does or might do for you. The minute you get your eyes on the problem, or on rewards or benefits you are expecting, you are no longer praising.

Some years ago when my kids were still at home, my older son borrowed our VW Beetle so that he and a friend could camp out on a Saturday night. They had promised to be back in time for Sunday church service, but the next morning there was no sign of them. By 1 P.M., I was driving up to our house, angry because the boys had not shown up, and fearful lest something should have happened to them. I managed to control my feelings though, and said to myself, "I'm going to praise the Lord. He's great and marvelous, no matter what else is happening." So I began to praise Him, at first feeling as though I was chewing dry oatmeal, but feeling better as I continued. As I topped the crest of the hill approaching our house I saw our little VW pulling into the driveway. The boys had had some problem with the car which had delayed them, but they were perfectly okay. When I had turned my mind away from the problem that had been worrying me, and given my attention to praising God, He was able to help.

Do We Praise and Thank God for Everything?

"You should praise God for whatever happens, bad or good. If you do this, everything will turn out all right." This is a very common teaching. Best-selling books have been written on it. I know what people mean when they say it, or write it, but it needs to be handled with care. If you tell me to "praise God *for* everything," you are telling me that God *causes* everything, bad as well as good. A lot of people think He does, but as I said in the first chapters of this book, I do not. I feel I'm on safe ground, because it doesn't seem from the Scripture that Jesus believed so either. I don't remember that Jesus ever praised God for someone having leprosy or being blind or lame. He certainly didn't praise God because Lazarus was dead! No, according to the Bible, Jesus saw these things as the work of the enemy, the devil, and the New Testament says "the Son of God appeared for this reason, that He might tear down the works of the devil."[6] Acts 10:38 says "God anointed Jesus of Nazareth with the Holy Spirit, and with power; who went through the country doing good, and healing everyone that was being oppressed by the devil, because God was with Him."

Besides, we just got through saying you can't praise God *for* anything, but only praise Him for Himself, for what He is.

"Well, then, you need to *thank* Him for everything. After all, Paul says we should give thanks always *for* all things."

It's true that Ephesians 5:20 in the King James Version says "giving thanks always for all things unto God," but the Greek preposition here is *huper,* which, used with the genitive as it is here, means "on behalf of." The Jerusalem Bible has a better translation of this passage; "go on singing . . . to the Lord . . . so that always and everywhere you are giving thanks to God who is our Father." I don't think Paul means to imply here that all things, good or bad, come from God, but that in whatever circumstances, we should go on thanking God for His goodness. In 1 Thessalonians 5:18 Paul says, "*In* everything give thanks: for this is the will of God in Christ Jesus concerning you." Everything happening is not the will of God, but it is His will for you to give thanks *in* the midst of everything, good and bad, for that frees Him to work in your life to defeat the bad and increase the good.

If, in spite of what's happening around you, you keep your eyes on God and keep on praising Him *in,* not *for,* the situation, you keep yourself free to receive His help and He can release His power through you to change the circumstances that are threatening you.

Praising with Others

It's highly important to praise in company with others. From earliest times, God's friends have come together to celebrate and praise Him. You can understand this from a human point of view. If you have a new camera or a new car, you look for someone to tell about it; you want to talk about it. If you find something fun to do, anything from collecting stamps to gardening, you want to get together with other people who like to do it too so you can talk about your hobby, share your enthusiasm for it, learn more about it.

In an infinitely higher sense, when I discover how tremendous and real God is, I want to get together with other people to share my enthusiasm about Him. The Holy Spirit living in me draws me into fellowship with other people He is living in so I find myself praising God in company with others. As I do this, because the Holy Spirit of God is in them, as well as in me, our common experience of Him is heightened, and the whole group can be caught up in the glory of God in a greater way than when we are by ourselves.

Isaiah saw and heard the seraphim around God's throne as they "kept calling to one another 'Holy, holy, holy is the Lord of hosts; the whole earth is full of his glory.' "[7] They're doing it in Heaven right now, and I don't think they're just carrying out a duty. It's just that they are right there with God, and He is so wonderful that they just *have* to tell one another about it, over and over!

One weekday morning my church librarian, a cultured, intellectual, and gracious lady, called me to discuss books. When I answered the phone I said, "Praise the Lord!" She said "Amen! Glory to God!" I said, "Praise God!" She said, "Blessed be His Name!" I said, "Amen!" and on and on we went, caught up in praising God to one another.[8] It was several minutes before we could get down to talking about books. After that, I felt I understood what the seraphim were doing!

When God's people get together, they want to praise Him to one another. As renewal in the Spirit began in my Episcopal church in Los Angeles, people started getting together spontaneously to talk about God and to praise Him and love Him. To love is to share. Love is not something you *have;* it's something you *do.* Your love for God needs to be shared. Paul says that if you don't have anyone else to talk to, you should talk to yourself about the Lord! If there isn't anyone else to share with, share with yourself! He says this twice in letters of his that we have. To his friends in Ephesus he writes, "Talk to *yourselves* in psalms and hymns and spiritual songs, singing and praising in your *heart* to the Lord."[9] And he says the same thing to the people at Colossae: "Teaching and encouraging *yourselves* in psalms and hymns and spiritual songs [this last probably meaning 'singing in the Spirit,' or singing in tongues], singing with gratitude in your *heart* to the Lord."[10] The Authorized Version translates the first passage "speaking to yourselves," and the second one "to one another." Most if not all of the later translations say "to one another" rather than "to yourselves," but the Greek word in both passages is *heautois,* which means "to yourselves" rather than *allelois,* to one another. That Paul in these places is encouraging people to talk and sing within themselves is further confirmed because in both he says this is something to be done not "from your hearts," but "in your heart." Why would Paul tell them to do this "in your *heart,*" singular number, if it was being shared with others? Clearly, the translators, both of the King James and of later versions, were not comfortable with the idea of Christians talking to themselves, even about God!

In a very cold climate, as in central Alaska, the temperature drops so low in the winter that even inside the house the water would freeze in the pipes if it were not kept moving. Therefore a pump is provided which keeps the water circulating through the system, even when it is not flowing out to be used for washing dishes, bathing, or drinking. This seems to me to be a good analogy of how we need to allow the Spirit of God in us to be moving in praise, even when we are not speaking to others. We can get spiritually frozen very quickly! Today, as believers are being set free once more in the Holy Spirit they have begun to understand what the early Church knew: that at those times when you cannot be together with others, you need to keep the praise of God going on in your own heart, and talk to yourself about the goodness and love of God when you have no one else to talk to.

From reading Paul's letters, we catch a glimpse of what the early Christians did when they got together. They usually met in private homes. "When you come together, everyone of you has a psalm, has a doctrine, has a tongue, has a revelation, has an interpretation. . . . Let two or three prophets speak, and let the others evaluate what is said. If a revelation is given to someone else, let the first one be quiet and let him speak. This way you can all prophesy one by one, so that everyone may learn."[11] It is clear that everyone was participating. There were various ministries: apostles, prophets, evangelists, pastors, teachers.[12] They were to guide and teach and keep order, but were not supposed to do all the praising and praying and sharing.

When the freedom of the Holy Spirit among Christians became weakened, however, these special ministers increasingly became the ones to do everything. Praise became formalized; the congregation gathered mainly to listen and passively receive. Ultimately the "pew" was invented, so that the people could sit in "serried ranks," as at school, or in a lecture hall. And this, of course, is still the pattern in most churches today.

Some response from the congregation is allowed. The liturgical churches provide specific times for people to respond with "Amen," "Lord, have mercy," "Lord, hear our prayer," etc., but if someone were to spontaneously say "Amen," or "Praise the Lord!" it would startle the congregation and distract the minister! Any free-lance response from the people is not expected and would be considered disorderly. The people are there to be seen and not heard! I have often told the story of the little deaf lady who came to church somewhere in Scotland, seated herself right below the pulpit, and adjusted her old fashioned ear trumpet so that she could catch every word the preacher was to say. The usher tiptoed down the aisle, tapped her on the shoulder, and said, "Madam! One toot, and ye're oot!"

I am not here urging that addresses be punctuated with a running fire of "Amens," etc. This can be very unhelpful and often is just a way of drawing attention to the "Amen-er," although an occasional heartfelt response to something that is said can be encouraging, just as one might say, "Hear, hear!" I am saying that, as in the early church, there should be a time for people freely to praise and pray, sing and share; and as folk become free in the Spirit, even in churches with highly structured services (perhaps especially in them, because they don't have as much fear of losing track of things—they've got a script to follow!) there should be more participation from the congregation.

Balance Is Needed

This calls for balance, and there must be common consent and understanding. I have had people brag to me how they spoke out in the morning service in their very stuffy and cold church, and felt they had made quite an impact! They did all right, but not the right kind! One of the very worst things you can do, if you are in a church that is very strait-laced, which you're hoping to help limber up, is to burst forth with a "Thus saith the Lord," a "Hallelujah!" or an "Amen!" on Sunday morning. People don't understand. It frightens them and makes them pull more into their shells. The parish of St. Luke's in Seattle was perhaps the first church of a historic denomination to be openly "charismatic." Within a very short time after my becoming pastor, a high percentage of the congregation had received the baptism in the Holy Spirit, and were enjoying the gifts in free prayer and praise together each week. Yet it was at least eight years before anyone brought a vocal gift such as prophecy or tongues and interpretation at a Sunday service. This wasn't because I forbade it, but because the people, in love, did not want anyone to be turned away because of strangeness in worship customs; yet the services were joyful, free and warm.

I told in *Nine O'clock in the Morning* how one Sunday after the 11 o'clock Eucharist, a young Roman Catholic couple greeted me at the door. The husband said, "We were kind of disappointed . . . we thought somebody would, er, speak in tongues, or—or something."

Then his wife said, "Yes, but those people certainly love God, don't they? I mean, you can feel it! I've never been to a mass where people were so worshiping the Lord!"[13]

"Oh, ho!" I replied, *"That's* what we wanted you to experience."

It takes sensitivity, intelligence, and humility to conduct yourself properly in a praise service. The rule of thumb, though, isn't much different from good manners or good taste anywhere else. Don't make yourself conspicuous. You're not there to show everyone how free you are, or "how to do it." Don't try to be louder than anyone else. Don't do things other people won't understand, or might misinterpret. Above all, remember you are there to love God and to love the people there with you. Whatever helps them feel loved and respected, that's good! Whatever may make them feel condemned, or shut out, that's bad. Here, as everywhere else, love is the test.

Going Out

One great reason we don't stay free in praise is that we forget to go *out*. We come together to be healed, forgiven, inspired, and renewed, so that God can send us *out* to bring more of His lost sheep back to the fold. The good things we receive as we praise and love God together must be taken out and shared with the lost and the hungry. There's an unlimited supply, but it isn't given to store up. It's like the manna in the Old Testament. You use up today's supply, and there'll be some more tomorrow. Try to put today's ration in storage, and it'll just go rotten.

Christians are like that. Come together, and then go out and share, and all goes well. Just come together, and don't try to share, and things can get pretty musty!

Praise is necessary to your spiritual health. You have a spirit, a soul, and a body. If you've received Jesus, the Holy Spirit is living in your spirit, but He needs to flow into your soul: will, intellect, and emotions, and He needs to fill your body too. The Holy Spirit wants to baptize, that is, drench, flood, soak, fill, and overflow every part of your being, so that you will express Jesus to the world in the things you do, the places you go, and in the things you say. If we "offer the sacrifice of praise to God continually, that is, the fruit of our lips giving thanks to his name,"[14] we accelerate the flow of life and joy in the Spirit throughout our whole being.

You don't feel like praising the Lord? Do it anyway. Say to Him, "Lord, things are not going well for me, but I know You are always wonderful. You have the answers for me if I will let them in to my life; but answers or not, I'm going to praise You! Praise the Lord!

The Psalmist says, "Seven times a day do I praise thee."[15] The various monastic orders developed their hours of prayer on this pattern. Try it! Try to stop whatever you are doing every three hours during the day and spend at least five minutes just praising God. Maybe get a watch with an alarm on it and set it to remind you! Time yourself to be sure you spend at least five minutes. It can seem a long time in the middle of a busy work day.

Our relationship with God begins and exists in praise and worship. God is wonderful beyond anything the human mind can grasp. If we even catch a glimpse of what He's like, we can only respond in praise. As we do so, the life of God is able to flow in us. The song writer says it truly,[16]

God is so wonderful, I can't explain,
But I can say "Glory, Hallelujah!
Praise His wonderful Name!"

Notes

1. The whole story is in the book, *Nine O'clock in the Morning.* See bibliography.
2. 1 Corinthians 10:31.
3. Psalms 67:5, 6 Coverdale, BCP.
4. Psalms 34:10 Coverdale, BCP.
5. Isaiah 40:31.
6. 1 John 3:8b literal Greek.
7. Isaiah 6:2, 3.
8. Bennett, *Nine O'clock in the Morning,* pp. 37, 38.
9. Ephesians 5:19 literal Greek. Italics mine.
10. Colossians 3:16 literal Greek. Italics mine.
11. 1 Corinthians 14:26–31 AP.
12. Ephesians 4:11.
13. Bennett, op. cit. p. 111.
14. Hebrews 13:15.
15. Psalms 119:164.
16. "God Is So Wonderful," Virginia Marshall, Word 1964.

5

The Question of Healing

Does Jesus still heal people?

Does God want to heal everybody?

Are there people who are sick or handicapped because God made them that way, or wants them to stay that way?

What does it mean to have faith for healing? What can get in the way of that faith?

Is it wrong to go to the doctor?

This is a day of spiritual renewal, and with it has come renewed emphasis on divine healing. A lot is being said about it, and a lot of questions like these are asked.

The first time I remember having any contact with spiritual healing was when I was nineteen, living with my parents in Campbell, a little town in the Santa Clara Valley of California. I was walking home from the church on a warm evening in late spring. Twilight was fading, and the scent of apricot blossoms was in the air. I was limping, because I had sprained my foot slightly, and it hurt.

A few months before, I had had an experience with God. I was sitting in my dad's study (he was pastor of the church) reading a book, when suddenly I became aware of God's presence. I didn't see or hear anything, but I was filled with joy and love. I had received Jesus as my Savior when I was eleven, and this was the same wonderful warmth I had felt in my heart at that time.

Following this, I began getting up early each morning, waiting to sense His presence again, and often I would do so.

I hadn't thought much about whether God still healed people; but that evening as I walked along, for some reason I said, "Lord, if You're really here, would You please take the pain out of my foot?" As soon as I had said the words, I stood still, because I felt a strange but pleasant warm feeling that began in my upper leg and gradually moved all the way down to my foot, which immediately stopped hurting. I walked the rest of the way home without any discomfort at all.

A Deaf Child Healed

My attention was next drawn to healing fifteen years later, when I was co-pastor of a large Congregational church in southern California. A woman called one day saying she would like to have her two-year-old son baptized the next Sunday.

"I want to ask a special request of you and the congregation," she said. "My son is totally deaf. When he was a month old he developed an infection in both ears. Because of his age it was difficult to diagnose, and by the time it was located and treated the hearing apparatus in both ears had been totally destroyed. The doctors say there is no possibility of him ever hearing. I dare not let him out of my sight. The only way I can get his attention is to stamp on the floor—he feels the vibrations."

I muttered some words of concern, and she continued, "You see, Mr. Bennett, the Lord has told me that Christopher will be healed when he is baptized."

Now I was really concerned! It sounded to me as though this woman was setting herself up for an awful letdown! What was going to happen to her faith if, as seemed most likely to me, the child was *not* healed? I began, as tactfully and gently as I could, to remonstrate with her, but she headed me off.

"I know, I know. I don't expect you to believe me. All I ask is that you and the congregation pray. I will have friends in many places praying at the same time. He's going to be healed. God has told me so."

Whew! I spent the next few days dreading what was going to happen on Sunday, but on Friday I came down with a mild case of flu, which meant that the senior pastor would be doing the baptizing. He was a kind and wise man. I called him and explained the situation, and asked him to please pray especially for the child's healing and to ask the people to pray, too. Then I rather put the whole thing out of my mind.

The middle of the next week, the mother called again. "I just wanted you to know, Mr. Bennett," she said, "that I took Chris to the specialist and he responded to the hearing test. The doctors cannot account for it, but they say he is recovering his hearing."

My Interest Grows

Not long after this I came into the Episcopal Church, where I began to be exposed still more to Jesus' healing. Largely due to the work of people like the late John Gaynor Banks, founder of the Order of St. Luke, the Episcopal Church has for nearly three-quarters of a century been open to believe that Jesus still heals people. The 1928 Book of Common Prayer included a service for laying on of hands and anointing with oil for the healing of a sick person, and the 1979 Book has an even more complete one.

I came in contact with people who were active in healing and began to read books like Agnes Sanford's pioneer work, *The Healing Light.*[1] As I went on with my work in my first Episcopal pastorate, I continued to see undoubted healings now and then. I remember two more babies who were healed as they were baptized. One of these had been born with a defective esophagus, and the day after the baptism the parents reported the child totally cured.

In 1953 I became rector of a parish in the San Fernando Valley in which there was a group of women who met faithfully to pray for the sick. They had a collection of prayers for various needs. They would go through their list of people who were sick, or had other problems, and read the prayer that seemed most closely to fit. The prayers were labeled with capital letters and I remember one of the group saying, "It seems to me that this person needs 'A' and a little bit of 'J'!" This seemed a bit cut and dried, yet their prayers often seemed to get results, and my interest grew. I began to pray regularly for sick people following the Communion service on Thursday mornings and on Sundays, and, as requested, in homes and hospitals. I suppose in the course of a year I and my associates would pray for several hundred people.

Why Not More?

Still not a lot seemed to happen. No one sprang up and flung away his crutches! Yet every now and then someone would definitely be healed. A long-time member of the parish was diagnosed as having a malignancy in his throat. The medical specialist treating him was a friend of mine, highly skilled in his field, and a sincere churchman. He called me and said:

"Dennis, Mort has a throat cancer. I'm going to have to remove his vocal organs. I need you to help me prepare him for it."

A group of Mort's friends gathered 'round him at the altar after the morning service the next Sunday. We prayed and I anointed him with oil.

Perhaps a week later, my friend the doctor called me, sounding as though he didn't know whether to laugh or cry:

"I just don't know what to say," he said, "All the signs pointed to cancer, but when I got into that thing in his throat it proved to be an infection. It'll clear up shortly."

Such healings were few and far between, but not less wonderful when they happened. I estimate we were aware of perhaps one person healed every two years out of the hundreds who were prayed for, but it was enough to let me know Someone was at work.

Healing in the New Testament

Jesus spent most of His time curing sick and handicapped folk, setting bodies and minds (souls) free from demonic oppression. He didn't usually begin by talking to people about God; first He healed them. For example, in John 9, the record says that Jesus and His friends saw a blind man sitting begging (v. 8), and without being asked or asking the man anything, Jesus went over, made mud with saliva and dirt, spread it on the blind man's eyes, and told him to go and wash it off at the pool of Siloam. The man obeyed, and his eyes were healed. He went home, and promptly got into a row with the Pharisees about Jesus, which led to him being thrown out of the synagogue. Later Jesus found him and asked, "Do you believe in the Son of God?" and the man said, "Tell me who He is, Sir, so that I can believe in Him." Jesus said, "It's Me that's talking to you. I'm the one!" The blind man believed, says John, and worshiped Jesus.

Jesus not only healed sick people Himself, He made His disciples able to do it too. He sent them out around the villages, telling them, "Heal the sick, cleanse the lepers, raise the dead, cast out devils, freely you have received, freely give."[2] "Heal the sick . . . and say to them, The kingdom of God has come near."[3] "He sent them to announce the kingdom of God, and to heal those who were sick."[4]

Jesus clearly didn't expect them to stop doing this when He left the earth; He told His followers they would be able to continue the work after He had returned to His Father. "If a man trusts Me, he will do the sort of things I am doing, only he will do greater things, because I am going to My Father."[5] Jesus explained that one of the reasons He needed to go back to Heaven was so that He could send the Holy Spirit "upon" them in a new way. The Spirit was already *with* them,[6] but now He was coming to fill them with power, and that would enable them to keep Jesus' work going on the earth.

You can see in the Acts of the Apostles that they did keep on driving out evil spirits, healing the sick, and raising the dead. Soon after the Day of Pentecost Peter and John caused a sensation by healing a crippled beggar at one of the Temple gates,[7] and it wasn't long before sick people were being lined up on beds out in the street in the hope that just the shadow of Peter would touch them as he went by.[8]

Acts 8:5–24 tells how Philip went to Samaria to tell them about Jesus. This isn't Philip the apostle, mind you, but another Philip, one of the seven men who had been elected to the board of the "widows' relief society" in Jerusalem. It seems likely by his name that he was a Grecian Jew, perhaps from a Greek family that had accepted Judaism. He had picked a most unlikely mission field—remember the Samaritans hated the Jews, and vice versa. So here is Philip, a Grecian Jew, going to proclaim a Jewish Messiah to the Samaritans! But they listened to him and many accepted Jesus. Why? The Scripture is very specific: "The people unanimously paid attention to the things Philip was saying, *because they heard and saw the miracles He did.*"[9]

Healing in Church History

Some would say this kind of healing only went on for a short time, and then stopped when the original twelve apostles died (some would say after the Bible was completed). If you'll look even briefly at church history you'll see this isn't so. You will see that people have been healed by the power of God all through the history of Christianity. Here are just a few examples:

Irenaeus, one of the "Ante-Nicene Fathers" writing around 180 A.D., more than half a century after the death of the last of the twelve original apostles, said, "Those who are in truth His disciples, receiving grace from Him, do in His name perform miracles. . . . Others still, heal the sick by laying their hands upon them, and they are made whole. Yea, moreover, as I have said, the dead even have been raised up, and remained among us for many years."[10]

Not later than the fourth century, the Apostolic Constitutions, in giving the form for ordination of presbyters, instructed the bishop to pray that the candidate be "filled with the gifts of healing."[11]

Coming down through history, you find references to healing in the lives of those people who came to be called "Saints" (with a capital "S") because somehow they had been reached by the gospel in its fullness. (I like to call these people "New Testament Christians displaced in time.") Father Don Gross, an Episcopal priest, writes: "Healing directly by the power of God was seen in the work of St. John of Beverly, St. Bernard, St. Francis of Assisi, St. Catherine of Siena, St. Philip Neri, George Fox, John Wesley, and many others."[12]

Martin Luther strongly believed that Jesus still answered prayer for healing. In a letter written June 1, 1545, he responded to someone who had asked for advice about a sick man. Luther counseled that several should call on the man, pray over him, recounting God's promises in Scripture, and then "when you depart, lay your hands upon the man again and say, 'These signs shall follow them that believe; they shall lay hands on the sick and they shall recover.'

"Do this three times, once on each of three successive days," Luther continued. "Meanwhile let prayers be said, from the chancel of the church, publicly until God hears them. . . ."[13]

The early Quakers recorded experiences of divine healing. Wesley was a firm believer in divine healing, as the following entry in his *Journal* will show, "Pain in the head and back, with fever, had to lie down . . . pain, pain and coughing. These words came to mind strongly: 'These things shall follow them that believe.' Prayed and called on Jesus to increase my faith and to confirm the word of grace. Whilst I was speaking, my pain vanished and the fever left me."[14]

The Pentecostal Revival

When the Pentecostal revival began in force around the turn of the century, one of its clearest signs was healing. There is no way to deny the cures that took place through the prayers of such as Smith Wigglesworth, the English plumber-turned-preacher, to name but one among many. The records of his life reveal a man of little formal education, but uncompromising faith and high integrity, who was the channel for many healings in the name of the Lord.[15]

Some laughed at Sister Aimee of Angelus Temple in Los Angeles, because they thought her flamboyant. There is no question, though, but that untold thousands received healing through her prayers, just as there is no question that she founded a very stable church which continues as an effective part of the Body of Christ today.

Continuing my own story, in 1959 I received a new freedom in the Holy Spirit, and became involved in the Pentecostal renewal in the historic church (which today is called the "charismatic renewal"). I began to see a lot of healing, not just when I prayed for people, but when they prayed for one another. I said earlier that in my church in southern California it seemed we would have an unmistakable healing every two years or so; but now in that same church, as people began to experience the baptism with the Holy Spirit, healings took place almost daily.

For me it started in my own family. My younger son, waiting to go to a birthday party, had been playing with the cat in the back garden, and got something in his eye. Even though his mother had removed the foreign object, it must have scratched the eyeball, because when I came home my son was lying on his bed in much discomfort, in no shape for the party. Quite spontaneously, I put my hand on his head and prayed silently, then I went on into the dining room. In a few moments his mother came in and reported that Conrad's eye was no longer hurting. About that time my son himself walked into the room. His eye had stopped hurting immediately, he said; and he went off happily to the party with his friends.[16]

My eyes came open on that one! This was really the first clue that the experience I was having with the Holy Spirit might have something to do with healing. I honestly had not sought the release of the Holy Spirit with this, or any other gift, in mind. Except for healing, I knew virtually nothing about the gifts of the Spirit anyway; I just wanted to get closer to God.

I have often told how, a few weeks later, I called on an elderly woman in the church who had suffered for many years with angina pectoris and arthritis of the spine. She was in bed much of the time. Said she:

"I've heard what's happening to some of you people at the

church, and I believe it. If you lay your hands on me I'm going to be healed!"

I did lay hands on her, not feeling any great faith, but she had enough for both of us! I left the room right away without waiting to see what happened, but the next week she came to visit me at *my* house. "See what I can do!" she said, and literally skipped 'round the front room! A year later she wrote to me in Seattle, "I'm 84 now, and I get a bit tired sometimes; but last night when my neighbor, who is 72, locked herself out of her house, I climbed in the window and let her in!"

It wasn't just me. People were praying for one another and they were being healed. Why not? After all, Jesus had said, "These signs shall follow them that believe. . . . They shall lay hands on the sick and they shall recover."[17]

Healing and the Gospel

In June 1960, as I said in Chapter 4, I accepted a call to become vicar of the church in Seattle. As people there were released in the Holy Spirit, we began to see healings, just as had happened in southern California.

The gospel is the good news that God wants to heal the world, beginning by healing His people in spirit, soul, and body. Both "holy" and "healthy" come from the same root word, meaning "whole." In the days of good Queen Bess Number One, someone seeing a rosy-cheeked, healthy youngster running down the street, might exclaim, "What a *holy* child!" "Health" includes a lot more than just freedom from bodily sickness. Jesus came to bring the world back to wholeness:

> Back to spiritual health, as the Holy Spirit brings our human spirits alive and into fellowship with God;
> Back to psychological, or soul health, as we begin to have the mind of Christ;
> Back to physical health as the Lord comes to live in his temples, our bodies.

God Is Compassionate

Jesus healed people first of all because He was sorry they were sick and wanted to see them healthy and happy and free from pain.[18] In Mark 10:52, Bartimaeus, a blind man, was begging by the side of the road when he heard that Jesus was passing. He began to shout, "Jesus, You Son of David have pity on me!" The other people around tried to shut him up, but he kept on shouting. Jesus stopped and asked what he wanted, and then healed him. Then, we read, he "followed Jesus in the way."

Sickness Interferes

Sickness interferes with what God is trying to do. A lot of devout nonsense is talked about the advantages of illness. It develops great spiritual character, we are assured. But this is a dangerous half-truth. Emily Gardner Neal has been one of the leaders in the healing movement in the Episcopal Church. She says:

Just as my belief that God does not will disease is unshakeable, so is my conviction that although saints most assuredly can be sick, saintliness and sickness are by no means synonymous. Much contact with the sick over the past several years has demonstrated to me beyond any doubt that generally speaking, illness does not tend to sanctify the sufferer, but quite the reverse. I have seen that physical suffering is not inclined to elevate the spirit, but in the majority of cases degrades its victims to a purely animalistic level where the only reality is pain, and the only desire its alleviation . . . if you are like most of us, Christians or not, and have ever suffered even a severe toothache, your chief interest at the time was probably in reaching the dentist—not the Kingdom. It is not difficult to understand then, how someone suffering the agony of cancer is more apt to focus his attention on his next injection of Demerol than on God.[19]

My own mother was crippled with rheumatoid arthritis most of her life, to the point she could hardly walk or stand, and was unable to open her hands or straighten her arms or legs. She conquered the disease psychologically and spiritually, and lived productively in spite of it. There's no denying that adversity made her a strong person. God will always bring good out of evil. Her handicap, however, kept her from relating to her husband, or to me, her son, the way she would have liked. The disease worsened shortly after my infancy so that during most of my childhood she was not able to pick me up and hug me. The result was that though I knew my mother loved me, and though she strongly influenced and formed me intellectually, I didn't receive the physical affection I needed and that she would have liked to have given me.

Her disease kept her from having more children, depriving me of brothers and sisters. My father waited on her literally hand and foot to the end of her life, but was obviously not able to have a normal marriage. He was a capable man, and she was a highly intelligent woman, whom people liked and related to well. But because of her handicap, and the fact that the churches in our denomination expected to secure the services of the minister *and* his wife for the one small salary they offered, my father was not able to advance, but remained pastor of the same small congregation for many years.[20]

Did God plan my mother to be handicapped? Of course He didn't. I know as well as you that if Jesus had visited our house, in His physical presence, He would have immediately healed my mother, and then what a celebration there would have been, and how different all of our lives would have become! God wants to set people free from interfering sickness, disease, and handicaps so they can more effectively "follow Him in the way."

The idea that God's people are benefited by ill health has been strengthened by a quite unscriptural picture of St. Paul which portrays him as a chronically sick man, dragging himself around Asia Minor attended by Luke the physician, who kept Paul going by potations and poultices from his little black bag!

If Luke was a doctor before he joined the apostle's company, nothing is said of him practicing his art as he traveled with them.[21]

And how could anyone read the record of Paul's travels and even begin to believe that he was a chronic invalid? This is how the Jerusalem Bible translates 2 Corinthians 11:23–28 (Jerusalem): "I have been sent to prison more often, and whipped so many times more, often almost to death. Five times I had the thirty-nine lashes [a man was supposed to die after forty lashes, so the law limited the punishment to thirty-nine] ... three times I have been beaten with sticks; once I was stoned; three times I have been shipwrecked and once adrift in the open sea for a night and a day. Constantly traveling ... I have worked and labored, often without sleep; I have been hungry and thirsty and often starving; I have been in the cold without clothes." *This* is a semi-invalid?

Then, of course, there's Paul's thorn. I have had people say to me, when they were sick, "Oh, this is a thorn in the flesh, like Paul had." I want to say, "How exciting! When did you get back from the third Heaven? Tell me about the marvelous revelations you've been having" because of course, whatever the thorn in the flesh may have been, Paul says it came because he had had such wonderful spiritual experiences and revelations that this "messenger of Satan" helped him to keep his feet on the ground, as we would say.[22]

Note, too, that Paul does not say he had a "sword in his belly," but a "thorn in the flesh," a painful irritation, but evidently nothing that threatened his life or mobility.

What was it? Nowhere in the Scripture is the metaphor of a "thorn" used of a disease; always it is used referring to people. For this reason many believe the "thorn" was the continuous resistance and persecution Paul received from his fellow Jews, and other difficulties and distresses he encountered as he traveled and talked about Jesus. I believe a careful reading of 2 Corinthians 12 will bear this out.

John Wesley was one of the greatest men of faith England has produced. He lived to be eighty-eight and was strong and vigorous to the last. He had very little illness in his life, even though he was exposed to wind and weather on his travels in a way that we later moderns can scarcely imagine (but Paul would have understood). In his *Journal* on June 28, 1784 he writes, "Today I entered on my eighty-second year and found myself just as strong to labor and as fit for any exercise of body or mind as I was forty years ago . . . I am as strong at eighty-one as I was at twenty-one; but abundantly more healthy. . . ."[23]

Smith Wigglesworth, one of the great figures we have referred to in the early Pentecostal revival, was born in 1859 and lived to be eighty-seven. He died without any preceding period of illness while attending the funeral of an old friend. In his early days he had a severe attack of appendicitis. The doctors said he was too far gone to operate on, but two friends prayed with him. He was instantly healed and went out on a job (he was a plumber by trade). When the doctor called and asked how Mr. Wigglesworth was, his wife said, "He has gone out to work." Said the doctor, "They will bring him back a corpse, as sure as you live." Smith liked to say, when telling this story, "Well, I'm the corpse!"

He once suffered much from hemorrhoids, but again trusted God, and was totally healed. When he was 72 he had a tremendous battle with kidney stones, but looked to the Lord and came through without medical treatment. At eighty-five he suffered what was diagnosed as a sunstroke, but recovered fully in a short time. From then on, as his biographer says, "in this state of spiritual and physical glow he continued unto the day of his homegoing."[24]

The Scripture tells us that we are to be like Jesus. "As he is, so are we in this world."[25] Sickness cannot be part of that likeness. Can you imagine the Lord Jesus even suffering from a cold? Can you imagine Him saying to Peter, "Oh, I've got such a headache! You fellows will have to take care of the people today. I'm going to bed." No, you can't, because Jesus was never sick. As a matter of fact, the New Testament has little to say about anyone getting sick, but a lot to say about them getting well! Trophimus was sick. Paul does not express great concern over his illness, so we may presume it was not serious. Maybe he had a bad cold![26] Epaphroditus was seriously ill and almost died, but God healed him.[27] Timothy had "often infirmities," which implies that he was subject to recurring minor illnesses—Paul implies it was stomach trouble. Maybe Timothy was like some of the rest of us and allowed stress to upset him. Paul prescribed a little wine as a healer.[28]

Spiritual, psychological, and physical vigor normally go together.

Paul says that Jesus will renew our minds.[29] Isaiah says that if we look to the Lord we will renew our strength, fly like eagles, run and not get tired, walk and not pass out.[30]

Healing is a sign to confirm the good news that the Kingdom of Heaven is at hand. This doesn't just mean "the Kingdom is coming soon"; it means the Kingdom is at hand, accessible. Jesus said, "If I with the finger of God cast out devils, no doubt the kingdom of God is come upon you."[31]

John the Baptist had pointed out Jesus as the Messiah.[32] Shortly after, John was thrown into prison. He evidently began to wonder, as the days went by, whether he had been mistaken about Jesus. Why, if He was the Messiah, had He not yet set up His Kingdom? Why was he, John, still in jail? So John sent some of his friends to ask Jesus, "Are you really the One, or do we have to wait for someone else?"

Jesus said, "You go and tell John what you have heard and seen: the blind receive sight, the lame walk, the lepers are cured, the deaf hear, the dead are raised up. . . ." These were the sort of things, said Jesus, that proved He was the Son of God, the Savior of the world.[33]

You'll hear people say, "Oh, we aren't supposed to look for signs; we're supposed to believe without signs." Did Jesus say that? No, not quite. He said, "A wicked and adulterous generation is looking for a sign, and it won't get one. . . ."[34] Whom was He talking to? The Pharisees and the Sadducees. There was no sense in giving *them* signs, for they wouldn't believe anyway. But the people who were ready to believe, they got the signs. The people like John the Baptist, who knew and loved God, but needed extra assurance, they got the signs. And for those who already believed, the signs that followed them made them able to believe yet more.

God does not refuse to give us signs to help our faith, if we are ready to believe. "Lord, I believe; help Thou mine unbelief" is a prayer that the Lord answers.[35]

Things like healing are not going to convince someone who has his or her heart set against believing. I watched a doctor friend of mine leave a room, ostensibly for a smoke, because he knew that someone was going to give convincing evidence for spiritual healing. So, lest he believe, he left! (Not too much later the Lord caught up to him, and now he prays for his patients!) A person not ready to believe, can always explain a healing away: it was "spontaneous remission," "wrong diagnosis," and so forth.

Does God Want to Heal Everyone?

Does this mean God wants to heal everyone? Some say no, not only does He not heal everyone, but He sometimes makes people sick and leaves them sick so they will grow spiritually, or for some other ultimate good purpose.

The best way we can tell what God would do or what God wants is by asking, "What would Jesus do?" Jesus said He was just like His Father. He said that if you had seen Him, you had seen the Father.[36] In John 5:19, Jesus says, "I tell you most solemnly, the Son can do nothing by himself; he can do only what he sees the Father doing: and whatever the Father does the Son does too."[37] What could be plainer? If we want to know what God the Father does, we only need to look and see what Jesus, God the Son, is doing. So let's look.

A Short Course in Healing

Take a short course in healing by reading the eighth through the fifteenth chapters of Matthew, especially noticing the "alls." Let me show you what I mean. Open the New Testament to Matthew 8, and follow along:

As soon as Jesus had finished giving the teachings we call the Sermon on the Mount, a leper came and asked to be healed. He said, "If you're willing to, you can heal me." Jesus' reply was immediate, "I'm willing. Be healed!" (8:1–4 AP). The next verse records that as soon as Jesus came into town a Roman centurion, an officer in the hated army of occupation, came and asked Jesus to heal his servant. Again Jesus didn't hesitate or ask any questions. He just said, "I'll come and heal him." The soldier was taken aback by Jesus' sudden consent and said, "Oh, no, I wasn't asking You to come to my house. I know that You can just give the order and he'll be healed." And Jesus, expressing amazement at the man's faith, gave the order and the servant was healed (8:13 AP).

Matthew, telling all this, doesn't stop to catch breath, but goes right on to tell how Jesus went to Peter's house and found Peter's mother-in-law in bed, probably with what we would call the flu. Jesus just touched her hand and she got right up (8:14, 15). And then comes the first of the "alls":

"When the even was come, they brought unto him many that were possessed with devils: and he cast out the spirits with his word, and healed all that were sick." Notice He healed *all* that were sick. The next verse explains why. "This is what Isaiah said the Messiah would do," says Matthew. "He'd take away our weaknesses and handicaps, and carry away our sickness" (8:16, 17, literal paraphrase).[38]

And so it goes, one miracle after another. In chapter 9, Jesus heals a paralyzed man and then, while He's on His way to raise Jairus's daughter from death, a woman touches the hem of His robe and is instantly healed. After reviving the little girl He restores sight to two men and delivers another oppressed by a demon of dumbness. And then, at verse 35 we have another "all," and two "everys"! Read this carefully, for it clearly answers the question, "Does God want to heal everybody?"

"And Jesus went about *all* the cities and villages, teaching in their synagogues, and preaching the gospel of the kingdom, and healing *every* sickness and *every* disease among the people" (9:35, italics mine).

Chapter 10 begins with another highly significant "all." It tells how Jesus called twelve disciples and "gave them power against unclean spirits, to cast them out, and to heal *all* manner of sickness and *all* manner of disease" (10:1, italics mine). And at 10:8 Jesus says, "Heal the sick, cleanse the lepers, raise the dead, cast out devils; freely ye have received, freely give." So not only did Jesus heal *all* that came to Him but gave His disciples power to do the same.

Chapter 11 tells how Jesus sends a message back to John the Baptist, as we have already described, offering healing as a proof that He is the Messiah. In chapter 12, He heals a man with an atrophied hand. The Pharisees are furious because it is the Sabbath, but Matthew says that as Jesus left the scene great crowds followed, and He healed them *all* (12:15).

In verse 18 again Matthew points out that Jesus' healings prove that the Spirit of God is in Him and that He is indeed the Messiah. Jesus heals a deaf and dumb man, and again emphasizes that He is acting by the power of the Spirit (vv. 22–30).

Then at 14:14: "Jesus went forth, and saw a great multitude, and was moved with compassion toward them, and He healed their sick." Matthew doesn't say, "He healed some sick people." He says flatly, "He healed their sick." The chapter concludes with a regular barrage of "alls":

"When the local people recognized him they spread the news through the *whole* neighbourhood and took *all* that were sick to him, begging him just to let them touch the fringe of his cloak. And *all* those who touched it were completely cured" (14:35, 36 Jerusalem, italics mine).

Finally, in the fifteenth chapter, after recording Jesus' healing of the Syro-Phoenician woman's daughter,[39] there comes a glorious summing up:

"And great multitudes came unto him, having with them those that were lame, blind, dumb, maimed, and many others, and cast them down at Jesus' feet; and he healed them: insomuch that the multitude wondered, when they saw the dumb to speak, the maimed to be whole, the lame to walk, and the blind to see; and they glorified the God of Israel" (15:30, 31).

Does God want to heal everyone? There seems to be no scriptural basis to believe anything else. Do you ever read of Jesus making anyone ill or telling them they were to stay sick? Can you even imagine Him doing it? Even death did not stop Jesus. We have at least three examples of Jesus encountering people who had died, and in no case does He say, "Their time had come. It was God's will!" No, He raised them up![40] Someone said, "Jesus was the world's worst funeral director. He broke up every funeral He ever attended, including His own!"

I guess at this point some may be saying, "But we've got to die sometime," and of course that's true, unless we are here when Jesus returns. (A dear old friend of mine used to say, "I'm waiting for the Uppertaker, not the undertaker!") Don't forget, though, that death is an enemy. Death came into the world through sin, not through God. God snatches us from the power of death. "Death is swallowed up in victory," says Paul. "O death, where is thy sting? O grave, where is thy victory? The sting of death is sin . . . but thanks be to God who gives us the victory through our Lord Jesus Christ."[41]

When I am asked to pray for very elderly persons, I still pray for healing, even though I don't necessarily expect them to live long. God doesn't want them to have disease or pain. You don't have to have an illness in order to die. Old people often die suddenly and without pain, sickness or disability, perhaps in sleep. Some seem to know the actual time, say good-bye to their family, get into bed, and die.

Notice, I am not saying that God *does* heal everyone, but that He is *willing* to heal everyone. Jesus had to leave many unhealed. At the Pool of Bethesda, only one man paid attention to Him.[42] The rest all had their minds on getting into the water at the right time. They weren't interested in Jesus, but this one poor fellow had been there 38 years, hopelessly waiting for a chance to be healed. Jesus was able to get *his* attention! Jesus could not heal people who didn't believe or who didn't want His help. He had a hard time in Nazareth, His home town.[43] "He couldn't do any powerful things there, except that He did lay hands on a few sick people, and healed them."[44] We have seen that during His time on earth Jesus did not feel He was called to heal everyone in the world. At this point He was sent only to Israel, although He occasionally healed someone from another nation. When Psalms 103:3 says of God that He "healeth all thy diseases," it is clearly referring to Israel. God wanted to heal Israel first, so that Israel could take His healing to the world. That's why God chose them. Most of old Israel did not accept the Messiah, so the promise passed to the new Israel, the Church of Jesus Christ, which of course includes believing Jews as well as Gentiles, in which there is no longer any separation or distinction between Jew and Gentile.[45] So Jesus says to us, "Go and tell everyone, heal the sick, raise the dead, heal the world!" Jesus empowered us so that we could complete the work of healing that He began.

God Has Promised

We shouldn't demand things from God—sometimes Christians can sound quite impertinent and presumptuous—but on the other hand, if my earthly father had promised me something, I would be neither impertinent nor presumptuous if I asked him respectfully to please do what he said he would do, and kept on reminding him until he did. Jesus says, "Keep on asking and you will receive . . . Everyone who asks, receives."[46] Three times Jesus says that if we ask the Father anything in His Name, He will give it to us."[47] He says, "If you live in Me, and My words live in you, you may ask what you want, and you shall get it.[48]

Notes

1. Sanford, *The Healing Light.*
2. Matthew 10:8 KJV Mod.
3. Luke 10:9 literal Greek.
4. Luke 9:2 literal Greek.
5. John, 14:12 AP.
6. John, 14:17; 16:7.
7. Acts 3.
8. Acts 5:15.
9. Acts 8:6, 7 literal Greek, italics mine.
10. Irenaeus, *Against Heresies,* Book 2, Chapter XXXII, Section 4.
11. *Apostolic Constitutions,* Book 8, Section III, XVI.
12. Gross, *The Case for Spiritual Healing,* p. 114.
13. *The Living Church* (an Episcopalian magazine), March 11, 1962.
14. John Wesley's *Journal.* Quotation is taken from Emily G. Neal, *A Reporter Finds God,* p. 18.
15. Wigglesworth, *Ever Increasing Faith;* Frodsham, *Smith Wigglesworth, Apostle of Faith.*
16. Bennett, *Nine O'clock in the Morning,* pp. 43, 44.
17. Mark 16:17, 18. This is part of the so-called "lost ending" of Mark, but whether it was part of the original document or not, it was generally ac-

cepted in the early Church. The note in the Jerusalem Bible says, "That Mark was its author cannot be proved; it is nonetheless 'an authentic relic of the first Christian generation' (Swete)."

18. Matthew 9:36; 14:14; 15:32; 20:34; Mark 1:41; 6:34; 8:2; Luke 7:13.

19. Neal, *The Lord Is Our Healer,* p. 73.

20. This, by the way, is an example of God bringing good out of evil wherever He can. Because of my father's being prevented from moving to a larger church, I was brought up through my late childhood and teens in the same little country town in a location which was physically ideal in those days, before the Santa Clara Valley was industrialized. This was, of course, much better for me than if we had been moving every few years. I went to grade school, from the fifth grade, high school, and college while living in the same area. Not many can say that nowadays.

21. It has been presumed that Luke was a physician from Paul referring to "Luke, the beloved healer" (Colossians 4:14), and because he supposedly used technical medical language in his writings.

22. 2 Corinthians 12:7 ff.

23. *The Journal of John Wesley,* p. 391.

24. Wigglesworth, op. cit.; and Frodsham, op. cit.

25. 1 John 4:17.

26. 2 Timothy 4:20.

27. Philippians 2:26, 27.

28. 1 Timothy 5:23.

29. Romans 12:2.

30. Isaiah 40:31.

31. Luke 11:20.

32. John 1:36.

33. Matthew 11:2–6, AP.

34. Matthew 16:4, AP.

35. Mark 9:24.

36. John 14:9, 10.

37. Jerusalem Bible.

38. *See* Isaiah 53:4.

39. Why did Jesus seem unwilling to do this? Why did He ignore her at first? Why did He keep her in suspense, and even insult her by calling her a "dog"? All kinds of explanations have been given. Certainly Jesus did not suddenly become unloving, nor was He expressing "race prejudice," because at other times He shows no such thing. He healed the Roman soldier's servant without hesitation and in more than one parable has a Samaritan for a hero. When He gave orders to His disciples in Matthew 10:5, He clearly told them not to go to the Gentiles or the Samaritans. This wasn't because Jesus did not want to heal and save the whole world, but because His own people had not yet rejected Him, and so they still had the promise of God that they would be the ones through whom "all families of

the earth" would be blessed, in accordance with the promises to Abraham, Isaac, and Jacob (Genesis 12:3; 22:18; 28:14). Also it is possible that Jesus had left the country to get some rest and realized that if He healed this woman's daughter, He and His followers would again be mobbed by people seeking help. As a man, Jesus had limited physical energy, as is evident in John 4:6.

40. Matthew 9:18ff.; Luke 7:11ff.; John 11:1ff.
41. Romans 5:12ff; 1 Corinthians 15:54b–57, KJV Mod.
42. John 5:1–16.
43. Luke 4:16–30.
44. Mark 6:5, 6 AP.
45. Ephesians 2:13–18; Romans 10:12; Galatians 3:28.
46. Luke 11:9 AP.
47. John 16:23; John 14:13, 14.
48. John 15:7 AP.

6

How To Receive Your Healing

It often looks as though divine healing is erratic, almost a fickle thing. A devout Christian may fast and pray for months, then travel far to a meeting led by some famous healing evangelist, and yet not be healed. A drunkard may come staggering into the same meeting, not even knowing what it's about, and be instantly healed. A friend of mine was handicapped from polio in her childhood and could walk only with canes and a brace. She also had a painful bunion on her foot. At a meeting she prayed to be healed; the bunion disappeared, but her paralysis did not. Why would God heal the bunion and leave the paralysis?

You may have been disillusioned about healing because someone near and dear to you is not healed, yet you know he or she really loves and trusts God.

If God wants to heal everyone, why isn't everyone healed who asks to be?

Some say, "God pleases Himself. He doesn't have to explain to us why He sometimes does and sometimes doesn't do what we ask Him to." Okay. God is God, that's true, but the Scripture says that

He doesn't vary. James 1:17 says He doesn't turn away and leave us in the shadows. God is often called a Rock. Rocks don't shift. You can build on them, and count on them "staying put." It seems much more likely to me that any variableness comes from my side, not from God.

Is It What You *Say?*

Is it because we didn't use the right words when we prayed? We prayed to Jesus, or the Holy Spirit, instead of praying to the Father in the Name of Jesus? I remember a man telling me that he tried an experiment. He prayed for a man who had arthritis in both legs; for one leg he prayed to Jesus to heal it, but for the other he prayed to the Father in Jesus' Name. He claimed that leg got healed, and the other one didn't!

It is correct to address our prayers to the Father, in the Name of Jesus, and in the power of the Holy Spirit, but I don't really believe that it is because of wrong phraseology that we fail to receive consistent answers to healing prayer. God is not like a computer, programmed to respond to certain commands which must be expressed correctly to get results. He is a loving and understanding Father who knows our hearts and wants to do us good.

Some say everything depends on our "confession." We will have what we *say* we have. Psychologically there's a great deal to this. I don't ignore or laugh at "positive thinking." Positive thinking and speaking can help us be open to be healed by Jesus. Jesus says clearly, "Have faith in God. For verily I say unto you, Whosoever shall *say* unto this mountain, Be thou removed, and be thou cast into the sea; and shall not doubt in his heart, but shall believe that those things which he *saith* shall come to pass, he shall have whatsoever he *saith*."[1] I have a lot of sympathy and empathy with those who teach that we should make a "positive confession." It's certainly scriptural. But I need carefully to remember that the controlling command here is "have faith in God," or, as it should be translated, "have the faith *of* God."[2] It's not the words that *I* say that have power, but the words that I say with the faith of *God*, which is in me.

Words are important; they are creative and powerful, but they must be used in faith, otherwise the Name of Jesus could become a kind of incantation. To use the Name without the faith is to invite the kind of calamity that happened to the seven sons of Sceva[3] who tried to exorcise a demon by using the Name of Jesus. Nevertheless, Jesus has told us to use His Name, and if we use it with the faith of God, both heaven and hell have to pay attention.

Is It Lack of Faith?

Jesus so often said things like "according to your faith be it unto you," "your faith has made you whole," "all things are possible to him who believes."[4]

Is it then simply lack of faith when people don't get healed? Here's a touchy question! It must be approached cautiously, for any answer can be easily and painfully misunderstood. How can I dare to say of an earnest and loving Christian, who lives close to God, "he is not healed because he doesn't have *faith*"? Yet God says clearly in the Bible that He will heal the sick. Jesus says that whoever asks receives. If someone asks and doesn't receive, then I must either say God is not keeping His promise, or that something is interfering or blocking from the human side. No matter how good and loving and close to God the person praying may be, I'd rather put the failure down to human frailty than accuse God of being unreliable.

If you turn on your TV set and get a poor picture, wobbly and wavy and covered with "snow," do you immediately call the television station and say: "There's something wrong with your transmitter. I'm getting a bad picture here, and I know there's nothing wrong with my receiver. I paid a lot of money for it. It's the best on the market, so it must be your transmitting equipment that's on the blink!" You know you wouldn't do that. You would fiddle with the knobs on your set and perhaps try to adjust the antenna. If that didn't help, you would call a repairman. It wouldn't even occur to you that the trouble might be in the transmitter; you would *know* it was your receiver that was at fault.

It sometimes looks as if we don't trust God to be as reliable as the local TV station. When we don't seem to get what we ask for, we immediately say something like, "I guess there's something wrong with God. He isn't sending the things He promised. He must have turned off His transmitter or there's something wrong with it." If someone suggests there might be something wrong with *us,* we get huffy about it!

As far as I'm concerned, if God promises me something, and I don't get it, the problem has to be at my end. Either I'm not open to receive what I'm praying for, or something is in the way. I'd better not say "Oh, I guess God isn't going to do what He said He would," and stop praying. I'd better keep on trying to find out what's wrong.

In *Charisma* magazine Pauline Harthern gives a good example. Attending a crusade in England was a totally disabled man in a wheelchair. Injured in a mining accident, he'd had to wear a full body brace for fourteen years. Pauline says, "He was a fine Christian who before the campaign began had been believing God for his healing." Many others were being healed in the meeting, including the man's wife. As he watched, he was saying, "I believe. I believe. I believe." He asked friends to pull him to his feet, and help him stand up, but he couldn't do it. Pauline continues: "Everywhere people were being healed. 'Why not this man?' I asked myself." The man was at the meetings every night, and then one night says Pauline:

> I spoke on forgiveness—forgiving others, forgiving ourselves, accepting God's forgiveness. I told about the miraculous results which I personally had seen take place over the years in the lives of others because they had chosen to forgive.... Quickly I led the congregation in a prayer of accepting God's forgiveness, forgiving themselves and others who had hurt them. Then I prayed for them to get set free of all resentments, rejection, hatred and so forth. Finally I prayed a general prayer

for the healing of various diseases ... suddenly there was a commotion. The man in the wheelchair was walking the aisle ... like a robot because of the braces, he got to the communion table and dropped to his knees with both arms extended heavenward.[5]

She tells that after the service she asked him, "What happened exactly?" He replied:

While you were speaking on forgiveness, I accepted every word of it, putting into practice what you were saying. Suddenly an intense heat flooded my body. It was as if I was on fire for several minutes. Then I was bathed in perspiration. I knew I was totally healed.

I quote this beautiful witness at length because it so perfectly illustrates what I'm trying to get across. This was a good Christian man, respected by his friends and neighbors. It would have been foolish to say he "didn't have faith." He had no idea what was standing between him and healing until Pauline spoke on forgiveness and he accepted that he might need to forgive. When he did, the barrier broke and he was healed.

God was not withholding healing because of the man's unforgiveness. The barrier wasn't on God's side, but God could not heal him until the man took the barrier down. It's easy to forget that we need to forgive our fellow human beings. Our broken relationships can keep us from receiving from God.

We should not say that someone "doesn't have enough faith." Faith is not a quantity of something. It either exists, or it doesn't. You can't trust someone or something a little bit. You either trust him or you don't. If your trust or faith is hesitant, it isn't faith. This is why, in Luke 17:5, 6, when the disciples asked Him to "increase" their faith, Jesus pointed them to the mustard seed. He wasn't saying that they only needed a tiny morsel of faith; He was saying that a mustard seed, tiny though it was, could do mighty things if it had faith!

Where is the faith lacking when people don't get healed? In God? Not necessarily. I've seen people fail to be healed that I *knew* walked much closer to God than I had ever done.

In the healing? No, we're not discussing "faith healing," but divine healing, God's healing. Faith healing is psychological, in which some physical change is brought about by sheer will power, or by suggestion. It certainly can happen, but it's not what we're talking about.

In Matthew 9:27–30 two blind men came to Jesus wanting to be healed. He asked them, "Do you believe I am able to do this?" They said, "Yes, Lord." Jesus touched their eyes and said, "According to your faith be it unto you," and they were both cured.

First, Jesus asked if they believed in *Him.* "Do you believe that *I* am able?"

Secondly, He asked them to believe that He could do the specific thing they were asking for: "Do you believe I can do *this?*" When He said, "according to your faith be it unto you," He wasn't talking about faith in general, but faith to receive the specific thing He was being asked to do, namely, heal their eyes.

I not only have to believe that Jesus is the Son of God, that He's forgiven my sins and brought me into His Kingdom, and that He has all power in heaven and earth, I must also actively believe that He can and will do the specific thing I'm asking.

Faith doesn't just exist. Faith is something you do. Imagine Peter, poised on the side of the fishing boat, saying, "I have faith that I can walk on water!" One of the other disciples will surely say, "Okay, Peter, let's see your faith. Get out of the boat!"

Faith is actively trusting. Faith is more than intellectually believing that Jesus can heal; faith is the very act of appropriating and receiving the specific healing. This is why a beautiful saint of God can fail to receive what God is offering, while the old drunkard I mentioned earlier can immediately get it. Something is interfering with the action of faith.

I said above that faith isn't quantitative—you can't have a "little bit of faith" in something. You either trust or you don't. But you can have faith at one moment and not the next, or you can have faith for one thing and not for another. To "grow in faith" means to become more consistent in believing, and to learn to believe in more ways. For example, I can receive healing for a head cold quite easily. I ask the nearest Christian, usually Rita, to pray for me, and the cold goes away! If, however, I get a cold on my chest (I'm thankful I rarely do!) I have a much harder time trusting to get it healed, probably because I am more afraid of it.

By faith we can receive healing from God for all three parts of us: of spirit, soul, and body. It's easy to have your spirit healed. When you receive Jesus by faith, the Holy Spirit comes to live in your spirit and He completely heals it.

Then the Lord begins to heal your soul, the psychological part of you: your emotions, will, and intellect. This process is what the theologians call "sanctification." It is a life-long procedure, but is greatly speeded up by the baptism in the Holy Spirit which Jesus, in Acts 1:4, 5, commands every Christian to receive. We often need special prayer for "inner healing" or "soul healing" so that the Holy Spirit can reveal hidden hurts, perhaps in the very earliest part of our life. We can then see Jesus there, and let Him heal. The healing of the soul is more difficult than the healing of the spirit.

It seems to be most difficult to get the body healed. Probably this is because the body is visible and tangible, and so it's harder to have faith for it. It's easier to receive healing for a headache than for a broken arm, because you can't see the headache and you don't know what's causing it, but you sure can see the broken arm! If, however, the doctor diagnoses the headache as a symptom of a more serious problem, and describes just what's going on, with X rays to back him up, it becomes more difficult to receive healing for the headache. A serious disease or handicap is harder to trust for than a lesser one, although it is no harder for God to heal a broken neck than a sore toe! This is why my friend was able to have the bunion healed, but not the paralysis. Yet I hope that instead of being discouraged or even disillusioned because the lesser thing was healed but not the greater, this smaller healing showed her what God could do, and gave her faith to be completely healed.

We in the West are soaked in materialism. Our culture accepts the idea that material things operating by physical laws are what's "really real," and that spiritual things exist, if they exist at all, just in the world of the mind and the imagination.

The opposite is the truth: the spiritual world is far more real than the material. The material world comes from the spiritual, not vice versa. In the beginning is God, who is pure Spirit. He creates and upholds the physical universe.

No doubt one reason there are outpourings of healing and other miracles in what we would regard as obscure and primitive places of the earth, such as the jungles of Mexico or Indonesia, is because the people there are unsophisticated and don't know enough *not* to believe that God can do what He says He will.

Finally, we need to recognize that we are living in a fallen world. God is working to heal the world, but it isn't healed yet. Our souls and bodies are exposed day by day both to the malice of our spiritual enemy, the devil, and to the accidents that happen in a world gone astray—what Hamlet called, "the thousand natural shocks that flesh is heir to."[6] Our only defense is to trust God, for only our faith opens the way for Him to help us.

When People Believe

Four or five years ago we began to hear a lot about people getting legs lengthened through prayer. For a while it seemed as though at any Christian meeting or conference I went to, someone was sitting in a chair having his or her legs prayed for. I groaned inwardly, thinking people were just kidding themselves. Then one night I was the guest speaker at a Full Gospel Business Men's chapter meeting. The president, a simple and sincere Christian, noticed I was walking a little stiffly. "Your back bothering you?" he asked.

"A little," I replied.

"Probably need the Lord to fix your legs," he said happily. "Come on over here and sit down, and I'll pray for 'em!"

I didn't want to hurt the poor man's feelings; he was trying to be helpful, so I sat down and stuck my legs out, resting them on another chair, holding my feet together. My friend pointed out that one leg was half an inch shorter than the other, but that didn't impress me. Any doctor will tell you it's very difficult to measure the relative length of legs, even with proper equipment, but my helper didn't know that, so he just started praying. He didn't touch me; in fact he stood a couple of feet behind me. As he prayed I felt my leg moving out, and since I was holding my shoes together, as the leg moved the one shoe rubbed against the other: squeak-squeak! I got to my feet and was immediately aware that the length of my leg had changed because I walked lop-sided for a while! My back felt better, too.

Another Christian businessman "explained" it all to me. "You see," he said, "God *always* answers this prayer for legs to be lengthened. It gives people faith for other healings."

"There's no doubt that it brings faith," I said, "but I really don't think God is just making a specialty of lengthening legs. What's happening, I think, is that people are believing for legs—opening themselves in faith for God to do something about legs." If it was a fad, it was a fad of believing for a particular kind of healing, and because people were believing for their legs to be corrected, God was able to do it.

Wouldn't it be neat if we had a few more "fads" like this and people started trusting God that way for the healing of other things?

What Stops Us from Having Faith?

What are some of the things that block this kind of faith and make it hard for you to receive healing from Jesus?

First of all, you may have been conditioned against healing. You may have been brought up in a church that actively disbelieved in it, and listened to a lot of preaching and teaching against it. There's a popular theory that divides Christian history into periods. What happens in one period or "dispensation" doesn't necessarily happen in another. God changes the rules.

According to this kind of teaching, the enduement with power by the Holy Spirit at Pentecost with its accompanying supernatural gifts was only a one-time experience, just for the apostles. Healing, speaking in tongues, and other gifts of the Holy Spirit are "not for today." They happened in the early days, and ceased when the twelve apostles died or, some would say, when the Bible was completed.

I cannot myself make this sort of teaching fit the Scriptures, because God so clearly says, both in the Old and New Testaments, that He never changes. "I am the Lord, I change not" says Malachi 3:6. And Hebrews 13:8 says, "Jesus Christ the same yesterday, and today, and forever." Then too, those who teach this way seem to pick and choose what's going to change and what's going to remain the same. For the life of me I can't see why they should maintain that salvation is for today, but not the empowering with the Holy Spirit, or why they should believe the gifts of the Spirit ceased but not the fruit of the Spirit!

Nevertheless, if you have listened to this kind of teaching, especially in childhood, you may have difficulty convincing your unconscious as well as your conscious mind to believe in divine healing today.

Does God Keep Some People Sick or Handicapped?

You may find it hard to receive healing if you've been taught that God keeps some people sick or disabled in order to help them develop spirituality, or so that their steadfastness under affliction may impress others. You may have been exposed to popular movies and books that present this.

I'm treading on tender ground. I have to admire the courage and faithfulness of a person who, though paralyzed or in pain, keeps proclaiming his love for God, saying, "I believe He planned it this way and I accept it." And yet—and yet—will it make people admire and love God to be told He would treat His child like that? It certainly shows that a human being can faithfully put up with a lot, but how does it show God's love and mercy?

Some people quote Job, "Even if He killed me, I would still trust Him."[7] Job's declaration gets translated into the idea that perhaps God would actually kill one of His faithful people, whereas the fact is that in the story of Job it is Satan who does the dirty work. If a human father habitually kept his children sick, feeding them a little poison each day, saying he was teaching them how to deal with trouble, would we admire that father? Would we long to be in his family?

Again, we need to ask, "What would Jesus do?" Suppose Jesus walked into the bedroom of the man or woman whom God is supposedly keeping handicapped or sick, or suppose Jesus met him or her sitting in the wheelchair? What would happen? Is it conceivable that the sick or handicapped person would not ask to be healed, or that he would have any doubt that Jesus would heal him? Are we foolish enough to think that he *likes* being sick or handicapped, no matter how much attention he may be getting, or how much he may be told how his example is helping people? Does he not long to be well?

Most of all, do we *dare* to think that Jesus would refuse to heal him—that Jesus would say, "Sorry, old chap, but My Father and I want you to stay this way."

We are often sentimental about the spiritual benefits of sickness and suffering. (Please read the Emily Gardner Neal quotation on page 80 in the previous chapter.) I'm not denying that people can grow in patience and love during sickness and suffering, but that does not mean God chooses such ways for them. Which do you think would bring the greatest glory to God: the person sitting in the wheelchair or lying in the bed, or that same person jumping up, totally healed, a living testimony to the love and present power of Jesus? The New Testament's answer is, of course, unvarying. It doesn't say, "He has given the lame and the blind the strength to endure their afflictions." No. It says, "He has done all things well. He makes the deaf hear and the dumb speak."[8]

Jesus is just like His Father and certainly did not leave people sick or handicapped; He healed them.

In John 9, the disciples asked Jesus why a man was born blind. Was it because he or his parents had done something wrong? Jesus said, "No, it was so God could heal him." And when word came that Lazarus was ill, Jesus said, "This sickness will end not in death but in God's glory."[9] Does this mean God caused that man to be born blind and live for so many years begging in darkness so he could be a sort of "specimen" on which Jesus could demonstrate His healing power? That, again, does not sound like a loving God. What I believe Jesus is saying here, as later with Lazarus, is something like, "Now, because I am here on earth, God can take these bad things and turn them to His glory by correcting them." They were a part of the purposeless evil caused by Satan, but now they have a purpose: to let God show His glory by turning them to good.

If you have the slightest notion that God might not want to heal some people, you will think there is a chance you might be one of those, so you will not be able to pray confidently to be healed. I know that whenever I "talk tough" about healing, as I have been doing in this chapter, people receive it. If I allow the smallest room for someone to think he may be an exception to the rule, he's not likely to get healed!

Some people say, "Oh, I'm like Job! God's testing me," and my reply is, "Well, God healed Job and He wants you healed too!"

The Healing Line

When Jesus was healing in Galilee or Capernaum, each person who jumped up cured—each blind or deaf person who cried out in delight as he or she received sight or hearing—created faith in the next person in line. If Jesus were walking the earth in His physical body today it would be the same. But because He works through you and me, and because we are by no means perfect, people do not have the same confidence when we pray for them. In fact, faith can actually be broken down watching a "healing line" at a conference, or watching people kneeling at the altar rail in church, because so many do not seem to give any sign of being healed. Each person that has hands laid on him with nothing seeming to happen, destroys the faith of the next, and of all those watching. It seems to demonstrate that God is *not* healing everyone who asks. But it's really because the people in that line, or at that altar, are a mixture. Some are ready and open to receive, some are not. Some have come time after time for laying on of hands just to get a little extra blessing—it can't do any harm, and it might do some good!

This is, I think, one of the reasons many healing evangelists try to get people to fall "under the power," because then at least the on-lookers see *something* happen that seems to show the Lord is work-ing, and that brings faith. (There's more to be said about "falling under the power"; I talk about it in another chapter.)

One of the most successful healing ministries in recent years was that of the late Kathryn Kuhlman. Miss Kuhlman may have suc-ceeded so well in part because she did not normally invite people to come forward for healing; she encouraged them to believe that Jesus would heal them right where they were sitting in the audito-rium. Then she would have them come and tell what had happened. The result was that people present only saw successful healings; they did not see people prayed with and not healed.

In Lystra, Paul saw a man *"that had faith to be healed,"* prayed for him, and he was instantly cured.[10] It is vitally important to know, as far as you can, before you pray for someone, whether he or she has the faith to be healed, and if you are confronted with a healing line, or persons kneeling at the altar rail, at least you should ask each one, "Do you believe Jesus can do this thing you are ask-ing? Are you ready to receive it?"

We have healing lines and healing altar rails, because we still suf-fer from "clericalism," which means that we think the work of the Church is carried on only by the clergy, or other special people. Or-dinary folk are just supposed to passively receive blessings meted out by the power-filled leaders. Yet in the New Testament Church *everyone* was expected to manifest the power of the Spirit.

Through the Pentecostal revival, and its continuation in the cur-rent charismatic renewal, the freedom and power of the Holy Spirit are once more available to all the people of God. When people began to be baptized in the Holy Spirit in my churches, first in Los Angeles and later in Seattle, almost at once they began to lay hands on one another and pray for big and little needs. There were dra-matic healings—like one woman who literally received a new heart, as the specialist later testified—or it might be something simple. At a prayer meeting, a woman might say, "When I was cooking to-night I splashed myself with hot fat from the frying pan. My husband came over and prayed for me, and look!" and the woman would display an arm or hand without a sign of burn.

I conducted an experiment several years ago. I had attended a meeting led by a well known healing evangelist and had seen many people healed. Folks came from all over the country to attend the meeting, because the evangelist was regarded as having special powers. I noted though, that she did not invite people to come forward for healing, but encouraged them to trust Jesus to touch them where they were sitting in the audience. Many were healed, and then came down and testified to what had happened.

Returning home, I asked the people at our church's prayer and praise meeting to do the same thing: just trust the Lord to heal them as they were standing together praying. I went one step further and asked them to lay their hands on one another and pray for one another. Then I asked those who had experienced healing to briefly tell about it. Several people raised their hands and told how they had been healed. I did some arithmetic: seven thousand people were at the meeting held by the evangelist, and about seventy at ours. I estimated two hundred people were healed at the big meeting, but at least six were healed out of our seventy. It looked as though our percentage of healings was higher than that of the large meeting with the famous person. Of course, some of our healings were small things like headaches and sore throats, which people in the big meeting would probably not have come forward to tell about. But even allowing for that, it was an eye-opener.

Often since then, on Sundays and at other times, I have asked people to pray for one another this way. It has scarcely ever failed that out of a group of perhaps two hundred, some six or seven or more will claim to have been healed, which means that many more may have been, because some folks are shy about speaking up, and some are cautious. They'll call the next day to report. "I wanted to be sure I was really healed," said one woman, "and I was!"

These are not *just* healings of sore throats and headaches. One Sunday morning one of our old-time members was recovering from surgery on her foot and was in much pain. She said the foot was instantly and completely healed as we prayed for one another. We have had church members healed of cancer during this type of prayer, the healing being confirmed later by medical examination.

In a Full Gospel Business Men's meeting in Everett, Washington, as people prayed for one another this way, a girl cried out in joy. She had come to the meeting with her arms and hands covered with psoriasis, and as we prayed, it disappeared instantly.

A Word of Knowledge

While we are praying for one another, as I have described above, we tell people to expect to receive words of knowledge. For example, one evening a man spoke up and said, "God has shown me that there is someone here with an abscessed tooth." I asked whether there was indeed someone present with such a problem, and there was. Then the man who had received the word of knowledge went and prayed with the woman who had the infected tooth and she was healed.

If you're at a meeting and you receive knowledge that someone present has a physical problem, say so, and if that person identifies himself, go and pray with him. If someone comes to you and says, "God has shown me that if you pray for me, I will be healed," don't hesitate. Pray with him and he will almost certainly be healed. God has been able to give him a gift of knowledge and a gift of faith, an unbeatable combination!

A Ministry of Healing?

Some do have a special ministry in healing. History shows that there have been men and women who have had as much as ninety per cent success in praying for the sick. Often these are people who have been wonderfully healed themselves, and so have a strong compassion for others, and a desire to help them in the same way. They seem to know how to let the power of God come through them to others for healing, so the Holy Spirit is able to manifest His healing gifts through them regularly.

Their faith, by the power of the Spirit, can sometimes sweep aside all obstacles and bring healing, even though the person prayed for does not have an active faith, or does not expect anything or know anything about it at all. Nevertheless, even though a person has a powerful healing ministry, he or she should always try to find out whether people are ready to be prayed with, and take time to be sure they have faith before praying for them. Even Jesus Himself was not able to overcome the active disbelief of people in His own home town. Matthew says, "he did not many mighty works there because of their unbelief,"[11] but Mark says "he *could* do there no mighty work."[12] Even Jesus could not break the barrier of their lack of trust in Him.

God Is Always Ready to Heal

You can postpone your healing by saying, "It just isn't God's time, that's all. He'll heal me when He's ready." This sounds very humble and submissive, but it is often really just a "cop-out" to avoid putting yourself on the line and trusting God! Jesus never stalled when asked to heal. He never said, "I'm not ready to heal you. Come back next week!" We have said that God has no purpose in keeping you sick. He wants you well and He wants you well right now. God does not keep us waiting; we keep Him waiting and then blame the delay on Him!

The Soul Needs to Be Healed First

I believe the single most important reason people do not receive healing is they have hurts hidden deep in their souls. We saw a woman literally jump out of a wheelchair, perfectly cured from several serious ailments, because Jesus was allowed to heal a hurt in her infancy. We saw a woman receive instant healing for an arm that had been crippled for years when she and her daughter forgave one another and old hurts were healed. In both cases, the people had known and loved God for many years.

I can be kept from receiving God's healing because of unforgivenesses and resentments buried deep in my soul, unforgiveness and resentment of which I am not even aware. The Holy Spirit can bring them to light, though, and Jesus can heal them.

This is something which everyone needs to know about, but it's beyond the scope of this book. Please follow it up. I've given suggested titles in the bibliography and I especially recommend to you Rita's book, *Emotionally Free,* which goes into the subject in a very thorough and practical way.

Some Really Don't Want to Be Healed

Have you ever been tired after a long stretch of unbroken work, and thought, "It would be kind of nice to get a light cold, or maybe an un-serious case of the flu so I would have an excuse to stay in bed for a couple of days." Did you ever in your school days wake up with a slight sore throat or headache and realize with a sense of relief that you had a good excuse to miss the social studies test you had been dreading? Do you think you would have welcomed prayer for healing at that point? So, in a much more serious vein, some people may think they want healing, but subconsciously they don't want to be well because the advantages of being sick or handicapped outweigh the disadvantages. Some people who would otherwise be lonely or neglected—while they do not enjoy pain or sickness—enjoy the attention it gets them. God often gets the blame because they are not healed, yet the block is certainly on their side.

A man or woman who for years has had a serious handicap may have become used to depending on others, and he or she has inner questions, "If I were healed, could I cope? Could I take care of myself? Would I dare be normal?"

Does Sin Keep People from Getting Healed?

Do people fail to get healed because they are doing bad things? The obvious answer would seem to be "Yes, if your life is not right, you cannot expect God to heal you. You must clean up your life first."

Oddly enough, Jesus never seemed to take this approach. We have no record of Him ever telling someone, "I'll heal you if you straighten out your life." In fact, Jesus never made any conditions for healing. All three synoptic Gospels record that He did on one occasion say to a man, "Son, your sins have been forgiven!"[13] but the man hadn't asked to be forgiven. In fact, he was brought by his friends on a stretcher and we aren't even told what he said or thought. One day Jesus healed ten lepers. He didn't ask them anything about themselves before He cured them, and it looks as though only one of them recognized God at work, and came back to say "thank you."[14]

Once He told a man, "Don't sin any more or a worse thing may happen to you," but that was *after* He had healed him.[15] There seems to be no example of Jesus making any condition for healing except one: that the person must believe. Since, as we've already said, Jesus healed everyone who asked Him, there seems to be no basis for saying that bad behavior will keep us from getting healed.

What a relief that is! If, before God will heal me I have to completely measure up to His standards and then come to Him and say, "Okay, Lord, I'm all ready. I'm now worthy to receive Your blessings!" that would be an open invitation to pride and self-righteousness. It would also be hopeless, for how can I be sure I have corrected all my faults, even if it were possible to do so? The idea that God won't heal us if we have something wrong in our lives can be used as an indefinite excuse not to trust Him for healing. "Oh, there must be some secret sin in my life I don't know about!"

But a "secret sin," doesn't mean something that is hidden from *you*. A secret sin is something that *you* know about, but you're not letting anyone else know about it, hypocritically pretending to be good when you're not. It's certainly true that you aren't likely to get healed if you're doing something like that. You've got to be honest with God.

Don't delay coming to Jesus, no matter what you are coping with in your life or what bad habits you may be struggling with. Don't hold off from Him. Be like the prodigal, who simply got tired of living hungry in the pigsty and decided to go home, still smelling of the slop bucket! I'm not saying it isn't important how you behave;

I'm saying that Jesus does not make good behavior a prerequisite to your healing. All He asks is that you trust Him.

What About Those Who Are Not Yet Healed?

I am well aware this is a heart-searching question. What about the person who truly believes God wants to heal him or her, tries every way to receive healing, and still doesn't get healed? If you encourage him to continue to pray to be healed, doesn't this mean he will be living in chafing discontent, waiting for the healing to happen and wondering what is wrong with him if it doesn't? Yet on the other hand, if he settles down to live with his problem, will he not be accepting his condition and stop expecting God to heal him? This is what makes well-meaning Christians encourage chronically ill people to believe their condition is the will of God. It's easier to live with that—if not physically, at least psychologically.

I've already said I don't believe God has made the person sick or handicapped and that I don't believe God wants him to stay that way. I've said I believe he should continue to look for healing and realize that if it's delayed it isn't because God is holding back, but because there is some kind of barrier still in the way from the human side, something involving human freedom of choice that God cannot break through. It may be a deeply hidden problem which he as yet has no way to unearth or it may be something more obvious which he can discover through careful prayer, thought and counsel.

I am saying that person should do everything that comes to his attention that might weaken or remove that barrier. He is without doubt trying any new medical procedure or treatment that comes along and will not necessarily be living unhappily if the latest medical therapy doesn't work. Nor will he feel guilty about it. So with the spiritual healing. It is being held back by something that needs curing, but until the difficulty is identified he doesn't know how to remove it. It isn't his fault and it isn't God's fault, and just as he tries various medical cures in the hope of finding one that works, and is not discouraged or guilty about the ones that don't, so he should be able to try various ways to receive his healing from God, and not be discouraged or feel guilty if he doesn't get the answer right away. But to stop praying about it, and say, "Well, I guess God isn't ready to heal me, or maybe wants me sick, so I'll stop trying to receive healing from Him. When He's ready, He'll heal me," is just like the same person saying, if a medical cure fails to help, "Well, I guess the doctor wants me sick, so I won't try any more. When he wants to heal me, he'll do it!"

The minute I give way to the temptation to say to a sick person either, "God will heal you when He is ready," or "God doesn't want to heal you," that person is going to stop praying for healing. Jesus told us to keep on asking, keep on looking, keep on knocking.[16] He said we should "continue to pray and never lose heart."[17]

Some things are very hard to trust for. It may be well-nigh impossible for us to believe God could do anything about paraplegia, or some serious mutilation of the body. If someone has lost a leg, could God grow them a new one? Can God grow new members for the body? Well, when Peter cut off the servant's ear, Luke doesn't say Jesus picked up the severed ear and stuck it back on. He says, "He touched his ear, and healed him."[18] But how it goes against our common sense! Can we blame a person if he or she cannot bring himself or herself to believe for it? And yet, I have pointed out how many people have received faith by watching a leg or arm grow out. I remember one morning at St. Luke's, following a morning service, I watched as one of my laymen prayed for a woman who had a short leg. As I watched, the leg grew at least two inches. In point of fact, it grew too far and had to be prayed back to the right length! The woman then had to go out and buy new shoes, to replace the corrective ones she was wearing!

Just as I am finishing this chapter, I received the latest issue of a Christian magazine telling of how Cheryl Prewitt Blackwood, Miss America 1980, experienced just such a miracle. Her left leg had been crushed in an automobile accident and was two inches shorter than the right one. The leg was restored to normal when she was prayed with at a healing seminar in Jackson, Mississippi.[19]

Stop and think of the modifications in muscle, tendon, and tissue, to say nothing of nerves and blood vessels, that are required for a limb to be lengthened, and then ask yourself whether it would be a much greater miracle for God to recreate a missing member. Is anything too difficult for God?

What Can Be Done?

What should you do if you are trying to get healed? Read books about it, especially the New Testament. (I have a list of recommended books in the bibliography.) If you are physically able to, go to conferences and seminars, not just on healing, but wherever you can build up your spirit. Believe for little things first, little healings, little miracles. Don't scorn them or say, "If God can help me with a headache or a sore foot, why doesn't He meet my real need?" Say rather, "If God can answer these little prayers, I know He wants to answer the big ones; I just need faith for them." As you receive answers for small needs, you will come to have faith for bigger things, for yourself and for others.

Don't let your own condition stop you from praying for others to be healed. As you see others helped it will help you to have faith. People have sometimes been healed themselves while they were praying for someone else.

Praise

Do we fail to receive answers because we don't thank and praise God for the problem before we pray? I've dealt with this question in the chapter on *Praise*. We do need to thank and praise God, not *for,* but in the midst of the problem. This is the most important thing to do. Get as close to God as you can. Praise Him, love Him, think about Him, press in to have fellowship with Him. Don't let your healing need stand in the way. Say, in effect, "I don't care whether I am ever healed, just so I can know your presence, Lord!" Everyone who knows God realizes that the sense of His presence and love is more important than anything, including bodily health, and any human being who has ever tasted God's love would have to say, "I'd be willing to be sick or disabled all my life as long as I could always know and sense God's love!" But be careful at this point. God would strike no such bargain and He always wants His love that delights your soul and spirit to break through to heal your body.

God Will Always Turn It to Good

God does not want us to suffer from sickness or handicap, but on the other hand, He will always bring good out of it, if we allow Him to. If you have a chronic illness or handicap, do realize that whether you are healed or not, God is going to bring you good, and while you are seeking your healing, God will show you how your problem can open the way to help others. Many persons have told how, while in the hospital recovering from surgery, they have been able to tell doctors and nurses about Jesus. Many have shared how, although they were not immediately healed, their unusually rapid recovery impressed the medical people, and gave them a chance to talk to them.

So an afflicted person on the one hand will know that God is not causing his or her physical problem, but also that there is nothing wrong with believing that God will bring good from the handicap or sickness, whether it is healed or not. This is not the best God has for him, though, and I would not want him to give up the hope and expectation that God will be able to bring the physical healing he is seeking. It may come when some unsuspected hurt in the soul is healed, or it may come when some person of faith is able to channel God's healing to him. And remember, the one who does that may not be some famous "healer," but may be a fellow-member in the local church, perhaps the janitor!

What About Children?

What about a little child, perhaps no more than a baby, who suffers terribly from some injury or illness and dies without being healed? How can we account for this? What barrier could be standing in the way in such a young and innocent being?

On the other hand, what reason could God possibly have for wanting or allowing a child to be tormented? How could the Savior who said, "Let the little children come to me,"[20] want a child to be hurt? Again, it must be obvious that He doesn't. We know that Jesus would allow no such thing if He were here in the flesh. The answer again has to be that there are things in the way which we do not know about. Even a very tiny child is not nearly as untouched and innocent as we fondly imagine. He or she has been influenced even while still in the womb by the speech and actions of those around, especially the parents, and soul healing may be needed before even a little child can be healed in body. (Rita's book, *Emotionally Free,* has a lot to say about this, and how to pray about it.) We must not stop our efforts to find these barriers and break them down, but in the meantime God will take tender care of the little one's spirit and soul, which He *can* reach.

Emily Gardner Neal, in *The Lord Is Our Healer,* tells the story of Kristin, a little girl of seven, who suffered for a year from sarcoma of the bone and ultimately died. Mrs. Neal describes how the child grew spiritually and touched the lives of many. She concludes, "The God I worship does not unspeakably torture a small child that her parents may know salvation or her friends and neighbors be 'inspired'! The God I love did not *will* her hideous sickness, but He used it. He did not *will* her agonizing death, but He sanctified her spirit in an extraordinary and wonderful way—and all of us who came within her sphere received a vicarious benediction."[21]

What About Doctors?

In the first place, a true physician is one whom God has called to heal people. If God wanted people to be sick, or had a purpose in them being sick, then doctors would be working against God.

If someone tells me he believes God has made him sick, is keeping him sick, or has some purpose in him being sick, I ask him:

"Then why did you call the doctor to help you get well? Why are you taking that medicine? If it were true God wanted you sick, you'd better be good and sick and get it over with! For heaven's sake don't ask the poor doctor to fight against God!"

Medical people who believe in God often have an easier time believing God wants to heal than most other people do. They know they are called to heal, and would find it strange if it were against God's will. There are a great many doctors and nurses who believe firmly in divine healing, and who pray for their patients. Rita's brother, Dr. William Standish Reed, is a successful and skilled surgical specialist. He has been involved in the healing movement for many years. He has established an organization called the Christian Medical Foundation which has over three thousand doctors on its rolls who are interested in divine healing.[22] Dr. Reed is the author of *Healing the Whole Man.*[23]

A close friend of ours, a leading neurosurgeon, before scheduling surgery suggests to his patients that they get healing prayer. If the person is a Christian, he sends him to his pastor. If it seems right to do so, he may pray with a patient himself. Then if the person doesn't seem to receive healing directly from God, the doctor picks up his scalpel and goes to work, knowing God will guide him.

One day I was talking about prayer healing with a doctor friend here in Seattle. He said with a grin, "Don't worry, Dennis, if God heals everybody I can always sell insurance!"

I replied, "That's all right, Bob, ninety percent of the world will still need your help!"

God heals the sick and wants to heal the sick, and as the renewal moves on and gains momentum more and more people will be healed directly by the power of God. But there will still be a vast number who are not yet ready or able to receive healing this way. This in no way reflects on God's wish to heal us, as we have seen. It simply means we need to find out what's getting in the way. In the meantime we may need to seek the help of the doctor.

Some feel that to go to a doctor shows a lack of faith and that you cannot expect God to heal you if you are using human help. This sometimes creates terrible situations, as when a child dies because the parents, determined to trust God, will not get medical help. This sort of thing causes people to look askance at the whole idea of divine healing. We do not condemn the parents in such cases; they have enough to bear, but they are tragically mistaken. We cannot make a decision like this for another person, not even our own children.

Give God the first chance, though! Years ago my younger son had an infection in his knee. I could see a red line gradually moving up his leg, and I knew things could get mighty serious if something wasn't done. I was ready to call the doctor immediately, but his mother said, "What's the matter with praying first?" I calmed down, remembered my faith, and we prayed. Several hours later, the leg was improved, but the infection was obviously still there. "We'd better call that doctor!" I said. "What's the matter with praying again," inquired the faith-full member of the household! We did, and the leg was completely healed.

Always pray first, no matter how serious the situation may be. Give the God of miracles a chance to show you what He can and will do. If no healing seems to take place, by all means get the person to the doctor, but don't stop praying. The miracle may happen at any point and the doctor may have a share in it. Pray for God to guide him and everyone who is trying to help.

If someone asks me, "Should I go to the doctor or should I just trust God," my reply is, "the very fact that you would ask my opinion shows that you should go to the doctor." The only time persons are justified in *not* getting medical help is when they themselves are deeply convinced that God is going to heal them. No other person can determine this. It is a gift of faith.

When Jesus healed the ten lepers (Luke 17:11–19), He said, "Go show yourselves to the priests," which was the nearest thing to the Health Department. In fact, apparently this was the act of faith Jesus required of them, that they would set out to show themselves to the priests even before there was any evidence of healing, because it says, "As they went, they were cleansed" (KJV Mod.). So when we are praying for someone who has been under medical care, when he is healed, we tell him "Go and show yourself to the doctor." We tell him not to discontinue medications, etc., until the doctor has confirmed that he has been cured.

Being Sensible About Your Body

No discussion of divine healing would be complete without saying something about proper care of your body. I believe God will heal diseases that are caused by neglect or abuse of the body. The miracle at Bethesda in John 5 seems to show that, because Jesus told the fellow that he'd better not do it again, whatever it was that had brought him to that condition. If you know better, though, and willfully continue that neglect or abuse, you are showing that you don't really want to be well. Probably it's because deep in your soul you don't like yourself and may even be seeking to destroy yourself.

At a conference recently a woman was present who was using an oxygen tank to aid her breathing. She said she was only given a short time to live because her lungs were in such bad condition from years of heavy smoking. She said, "There's no use in me asking to be healed, because even if God healed me I'd go right back to smoking!"

At least she was honest, and of course her problem was she needed her soul healed from whatever was driving her to smoke, even though it was killing her. And there are people who behave as she did, only in less dramatic ways. What about the "junk food junkies" and the over-weights? Or those who take no exercise? Often the long-term results are blamed on God.

There are always plenty of health fads going around, of course, but one thing upon which there seems to be general agreement is the importance of exercise. There's a wide disagreement about vitamins and other food supplements, but proper nutrition is vitally important. I can testify that since my wife, Rita, began to study proper nutrition some years ago and make sure that we had the right vitamins and minerals in our diet, I have noticed a definite increase in my general stamina. I do not see the vitamins and minerals I take as "medicine" but as part of my regular food. I'm no "spring chicken," but I run two miles at least three times a week with no difficulty!

In Conclusion

God is not glorified in sickness and death. He is glorified in life and health. Jesus was never sick and never indicated in any way that sickness was part of His plan. I cannot claim sickness as identification with Jesus' sufferings, for He did not suffer from ill health.

If we really mean what we say when we pray, "Thy Kingdom come on earth as it is in Heaven," we cannot believe that God wants sickness to continue on earth for any reason whatsoever, for in Heaven there is no sorrow, nor sighing, nor any pain.[24] When the Kingdom comes fully on earth, sickness and sorrow and pain will disappear. God is already establishing His Kingdom on the earth as people receive Jesus and are filled with the Holy Spirit. Luke 17:21 was mistranslated in the King James Bible, if we may say such a thing about a much beloved verse. Jesus did not say, "The Kingdom of God is within you," although that is certainly true of a person who has received the Lord; but Jesus was talking to the Pharisees. What He said was, "The Kingdom of God is *among* you,"[25] that is, the Kingdom of Heaven has begun to come on the earth right in your midst, whether you recognize it or not, and whether you like it or not. The Kingdom is already beginning to be established on earth wherever there are those who are letting the power of the Holy Spirit be expressed through them; and when the Kingdom comes, sickness has to leave. You may be enjoying the Kingdom of God in your spirit and you may be receiving healing and peace in your soul, but don't forget that God wants to heal your body too.

Pray for the sick: anyone, any time, anywhere, as Jesus leads you. Don't wait for the "experts" or feel that you have no right to do this kind of thing. Jesus said, "These signs shall follow *them that believe.*"[26]

Don't be afraid to ask others to pray for you, and remember, some people are healed as they forget about their own needs and pray for someone else. Think about the part of you that is whole. If you've received Jesus, your Spirit is joined to God and is perfectly well. Let His wholeness and His Kingdom be released into the rest of your being and then ask to bless others. Most of all, right where you are and as you are, seek to know and enjoy God's presence more fully.

You pray, "Thy Kingdom come," so let it begin to happen, more and more.

Notes

1. Mark 11:22, 23, italics mine.
2. KJV margin, literal Greek.
3. Acts 19:14.
4. Matthew 9:22, 29; Mark 9:23 KJV Mod.
5. Pauline Harthern, "Forgiveness Brought a Miracle," *Charisma,* February 1982, p. 20.
6. *Hamlet,* Act III, Sc. 1.
7. Job 13:15 AP.
8. Mark 7:37 KJV Mod.
9. John 11:4 Jerusalem Bible.
10. Acts 14:8.
11. Matthew 13:58.
12. Mark 6:5, italics mine.
13. Matthew 9:1-8; Mark 2:1-12; Luke 5:17-26, literal Greek.
14. Luke 17:12-19.
15. John 5:14 AP.
16. Matthew 7:7, 8, literal Greek paraphrase.
17. Luke 18:1 AP.
18. Luke 22:51.
19. Sherry Andrews, "The Courtship of Cheryl Prewitt and Terry Blackwood," *Charisma,* February 1982, pp. 25-31.
20. Mark 10:14 Jerusalem Bible.
21. Neal, *op. cit.,* p. 83.
22. For information write to Christian Medical Foundation, Inc., P.O. Box 15835, Tampa, FL 33614.
23. Reed, *Healing the Whole Man,* originally published as, *Surgery of the Soul.*

24. Revelation 21:3–7.

25. Jerusalem Bible.

26. Mark 16:17, italics mine. See note 17 of the previous chapter about the "lost ending" of this Gospel.

7

Creation and Evolution

A lot of people think the universe came about by accident. It's not a new idea. Five hundred years before Christ, the Greek philosopher Leucippus and his disciple Democritus, taught that the whole of reality was only a swarm of atoms in space. As these swirled around they got into all conceivable shapes and patterns, so that as time went by, all possible kinds of worlds came into existence and passed out of existence, purely by accident, without any plan or meaning, like faces in the fire or figures in the clouds.

If the whole world could come about by accident, I should be able to build a house the same way, provided I have unlimited time to do it. So I'll gather the lumber, glass, plumbing, nails, pipe, plaster, and the rest of the material needed. To keep the pull of gravity from interfering, I'll collect all this together somewhere out in space. Then I'll get a few husky gorillas, put them in space suits, equip them with space bulldozers, shovels, hammers, and so forth, and set them to work pushing my collection of building materials around at random, hammering on it, stirring it, throwing it. If they keep this up long enough, sooner or later, if the "accidentalists" are right, the stuff will assemble, purely by chance, into the exact house I have in mind. In fact, I don't even need to decide ahead of time what sort of house I want, because if I will just observe the process as the ages go by, all possible different kinds of houses will come together at different times. When the one I want turns up, I'll stop things at that point, tow my house back to earth, and move in!

What Would Really Happen?

You know what would really happen to my conglomeration of building material, don't you? It wouldn't ever turn into a house, not in a million trillion years. As the workers stirred it around, it would get more and more broken down and scattered; and in far less than a million years—probably within just a few days—all I'd have would be splinters and dust, and that mass of splinters and dust would get more and more splintery and dusty and scattered as time went by. It would never re-form itself accidentally even into two-by-fours and bathtubs, let alone a complete house!

Notice, too, I started my house-building project with partially assembled things: lumber, plumbing, and glass. For a truly accidental house, I would need to start with a mass of totally formless stuff and expect it to come together into windows, kitchen cabinets, fireplaces, and so forth!

The "accidentalists" seem to think, though, that I would eventually get my house, because they believe life was created by accident in the primeval ocean. Several years ago, speaking of research being done under the direction of Nobel Prizewinner Dr. Harold Urey, *Time* magazine reported,

> Many scientists think that life appeared on earth when the atmosphere, instead of being its present mixture of oxygen, nitrogen and carbon dioxide, contained methane, ammonia, and hydrogen. These ingredients, still to be found in the atmospheres of Jupiter and Saturn, slowly combined into larger and larger organic (carbon-containing) molecules, according to the hypothesis. At last one molecule, a complex protein, showed

the ability to absorb other molecules and create replicas of itself out of their material. This "Adam molecule" was the first life; it could grow and reproduce itself.[1]

The article went on to describe how one of Urey's students, Stanley L. Miller, had simulated conditions on a primitive earth and managed to create several organic compounds close to proteins.

Miller set up a closed apparatus containing water, methane, ammonia and hydrogen. When the water was heated, its vapor circulated the other gases past a small electric "corona" discharge, which promoted chemical reactions among their molecules. . . . After a week, Student Miller analyzed the mixture. It proved to contain at least three amino acids. . . . This was the hoped-for payoff: amino acids are the building blocks of which proteins are made.

Professor Urey and Student Miller do not believe that they have created life. What they have done is to prove that complex organic compounds found in living matter can be formed, by chemical reactions, out of the gases that were probably common in the earth's first atmosphere. If their apparatus had been as big as the ocean, and if it had worked for a million years instead of one week, it might have created something like the first living molecule.

Now, suppose that in the course of my attempt at accidental house-building, after the workmen have stirred my pile of building materials for a day or two, a couple of boards have fallen on a nail and become fastened together, or two pieces of pipe have accidentally been screwed together. At this point I exclaim, "See! That proves that if we only keep on long enough, I'll get my house! We're on the track!" About this time, along comes a bulldozer and breaks apart the boards, a big hammer smashes the pipes, and my project is back to "square one"! And that is exactly what would have happened to the molecules in the primeval soup kitchen, if only accidental influences were at work. The same forces that accidentally brought them together, would have accidentally torn them apart.

To prevent this, in the Miller experiment, the amino acids and other compounds formed were immediately isolated by a trap from the chamber where the gases were being exposed to the electrical discharge. If they had not been, the same electric corona which created them would have destroyed them.[2]

With my house building project, this would have been just as if, when I saw a couple of boards or pipes joined by accident, I immediately set them aside, out of the way, so they would not be torn apart again. In time this way I would accumulate a collection of partially assembled things, but where would I go from there? I am nowhere near having a house, and if I throw them back into the melee, they will just be destroyed. So the fact that Miller was able to trap out a collection of molecules that could be used as parts of living cells proves little or nothing about the accidental creation of life.

It is simply not true that if you have matter in motion, and enough time, anything and everything will come into being, just by accident. Accidents don't work like that.

A Way to Clean Up a Mess?

Accidents fall down, not up. If you drop an egg out of the refrigerator you get a mess on the kitchen floor! The "accidental universe" theory says that if you take a mess, and stir and slosh it around enough, it will at some point become an egg!

Suppose you were shown a slow-motion movie which began with the smashed egg on the kitchen floor, and as you watched, the white and yolk gathered themselves up and separated themselves out. Then bits of eggshell collected themselves and put themselves back together around the rest, until there was a nice neat egg again. Finally the whole thing leaped up in defiance of gravity, and nestled back snugly into the egg tray in the fridge. "Aha!" you would say, "You're playing that movie backwards!" You know things just don't happen like that by accident. Humpty Dumpty accidentally fell off the wall, and broke into a thousand pieces! If the king's horses and the king's men couldn't put Humpty Dumpty back together, it's a sure thing he wouldn't, by accident, reassemble, and fall back up onto the wall!

Enter Entropy

Things left to themselves become more disordered as time goes by. This principle, called *entropy,* is derived from the second law of thermodynamics, which Albert Einstein called the premier law of all science, and Sir Arthur Eddington referred to as the supreme metaphysical law of the entire universe.[3] In fact, one of the ways physicists can give time an "arrow"—that is, know which direction it is moving—is to look for increasing disorder. I can apply this in my garage. If I leave it alone, it always gets messier and dirtier and more disordered. It never gets cleaner and more orderly as time goes by!

Sorting the Silverware

But now suppose that, instead of an egg, a drawer of knives, forks, and spoons has been dropped on the kitchen floor and you are viewing a movie of that event. Again, if you saw the pieces of silverware sorting themselves out, and climbing back into the drawer, and the drawer putting itself back into its place, you would know the movie was in reverse. If, however, you could see that the lady of the house was picking up the pieces, sorting them out, and putting the drawer back, the movie wouldn't need to be going backwards, even though things were becoming more orderly, because now there was *someone* organizing them.

There's Got to Be an Organizer

If things are becoming more orderly with the passing of time, it cannot be happening by accident. Someone must be organizing them.

The people who believe the universe came about by accident say that it began with a formless blob of undifferentiated matter, which, according to current theory, blew up with a "big bang." As time went by, various atoms formed, then molecules and chemical compounds. Later on, larger and larger molecules came together, and then life appeared. Living things in turn became more and more complex, until the higher animals came into existence, then human beings. And all this is supposed to have happened purely by accident with no plan behind it.

It is just as impossible for the world to have come about this way as for the smashed egg to have put itself back together again, or for the knives and forks to have sorted themselves out and climbed back into the drawer. It is against one of the most basic principles of nature. In order for there to be increasing order and organization, there *has* to be an organizer, someone intelligent and purposeful directing things. *It cannot possibly happen by accident.*

A group of molecules sloshing around in the primeval ocean are not going to come together accidentally to form the complexity of a living cell, any more than my building materials would form into a house by accident. But, if there's an organizer, then the universe could have begun as formless matter and gradually become more and more structured and meaningful, because Someone was working with it. And this is exactly what the Bible says happened. According to Genesis, God created formless matter, "the earth was without form and void,"[4] and then began to organize it. First God made light, then water, then earth, then vegetable life, then animal life. Believers differ as to how long the process took, whether the Scripture means six literal solar days, or a much longer period, but the Bible makes it clear that it didn't happen instantaneously, but over a period of time.

A Look at the Scripture

Note, too, that according to Genesis, God did not make living things instantaneously. He put the potential for the development of life into the earth and water, and then told *them* to bring it forth. Look at these familiar passages:

And God said, *Let the earth bring forth* grass, the herb yielding seed, and the fruit tree yielding fruit after his kind, whose seed is in itself, upon the earth: and it was so. *And the earth brought forth* grass, and herb yielding seed after his kind, and the tree yielding fruit, whose seed was in itself, after his kind: and God saw that it was good. (Genesis 1:11, 12, italics mine)

And God said, *Let the waters bring forth* abundantly the moving creature that hath life, and fowl that may fly above the earth in the open firmament of heaven. And God created great whales, and every living creature that moveth, *which the waters brought forth abundantly,* after their kind, *and every winged fowl after his kind:* and God saw that it was good. (Genesis 1:20, italics mine)[5]

And God said, *Let the earth bring forth* the living creature after his kind, cattle, and creeping things, and beast of the earth after his kind: and it was so. (Genesis 1:24, italics mine)

Do you see? It says the *earth* and the *water* "brought forth." The materialists imagine that this happened by accident, but that is impossible. God, the Organizer, put into them the ability to "bring forth," to organize formless matter into living things, and they began to do it when and as He told them to.

This is what evolution really means. It is quite inaccurate to speak of blind, accidental development as evolution. The word means to "bring out what is in you." The Latin verb from which "evolution" is derived means unrolling a scroll to reveal what has been written on it. When the earth and the water "brought forth" various kinds of life, they were "evolving" what had been written in them by the Author of life.[6] So, properly understood, instead of being a support for atheism, the concept of evolution, that the universe became more orderly and organized as time went by, is absolute proof that there is a God.

Why Do It This Way?

If, in creating life, God gave the water and the earth the chance to respond, this was because, as we have seen, He puts a high value on freedom. He would want to allow even earth and water the chance to obey Him freely, rather than forcing them to do His will.

A brief article in the *Reader's Digest* for February 1982 (pp. 130, 131), quoting *Newsweek* magazine,* talks about Spirit Lake at the foot of Mount St. Helens, the volcano that erupted violently in May 1981:

> Scientists from Oregon State University have discovered microorganisms in the lake that may resemble the first creatures that appeared on the primordial earth. The volcano's heat ... could convert primitive gases into proteins and macromolecules—the first steps toward life. The blast deposited metals and sulfur in the lake and heated sulfur-coated rocks in the volcano's crater to 194 degrees Fahrenheit—just the right conditions for the strange bacteria to thrive in. The microbes absorb food through their porous skins, feeding on iron, magnesium, ammonia, carbon monoxide and sulfur. Some live without oxygen, as scientists suspect the first bacteria on Earth did.... The Spirit Lake microorganisms are also similar to chemical-eating bacteria discovered in hot underwater plumes off the Galapagos Islands.

The article goes on,

> That coincidence suggests that such hydrothermal vents may have been the original caldrons of life. Sidney Fox of the University of Miami has simulated the conditions peculiar to thermal vents, with intriguing results. He finds that amino acids, the simple building blocks of proteins, combine into protein-like molecules in minutes and into bacterialike blobs in less than 24 hours. By studying these molecules and the creatures

of Spirit Lake, scientists may soon have a clearer idea of how life began.

Most people who read this undoubtedly saw it as further "proof" that life came about by accident. But that's because we are conditioned that way. Now let's think a little more carefully. This is a magazine article, not a scientific treatise. Presuming the facts to be accurate, if the molecules came together so quickly in Fox's concoctions, and, as is implied, if actual primitive organisms formed in Spirit Lake or in the Galapagos plumes in such a short time *neither could have come about by accident.*

Even those scientists who believe that life started when atoms and molecules came together accidentally in the primeval ocean admit that the process would have taken untold millions of years. Are we then being asked to believe that life started by accident all over again in Spirit Lake, in just a few short months? And that it happened *again* in the Galapagos plumes? Are the "bacterialike" blobs forming in Dr. Fox's flasks coming together by accident? The scientists simply can't be saying to us, "Look, the accident's happening again!" and certainly not that the "accident" happens wherever there is a thermal vent or a volcanic lake!

If the results of Fox's experiment, or the happenings at Spirit Lake or in the Galapagos Islands are being validly interpreted, they don't prove that the world came about by accident at all—they demonstrate what the Bible says, that there is something in earth and water that causes it to come together in ways that go against entropy, *against* accident. If the results of these experiments are accurate, they would show that matter is in some way predisposed to develop itself against chance, and that therefore there must be an organizing Intelligence behind it. In other words, God put the potential to "bring forth" into the earth and sea, and they're still doing it! God said to the primeval ocean, "Bring forth!" When the Lord Jesus walked on the water, the disciples exclaimed, "Even the winds and the sea obey him."[7] And it's still obeying Him! The water in Spirit Lake, and the water in Fox's laboratory flasks must still be responding to the command of God first given in the dawn of creation.

If the results of Fox's experiment, or of the investigations at Spirit Lake and Galapagos, are valid they are an exciting proof for modern man of the existence of God, and the reliability of the Scripture record.

If we Christians will stop being afraid and defensive, we will see that more and more the facts being revealed by science are supporting belief in God. You may not need such proofs, if you have met the Lord, but a lot of people would like to believe, but have been held back by the supposed "proofs" of science that the world came about without a Creator. It's important for them to hear the truth.

The Creation of Man

But God did not just create the cosmos, and then go away and leave it to itself. It isn't enough for there to be an Organizer—there also has to be a Maintainer, Someone keeping things going properly. God intended, I believe, as I have suggested elsewhere in this book, to keep in close contact with His creation and to see that the earth "brought forth" rightly, and to correct any errors that might occur along the way. He intended to function, so to speak, as a gardener who plants seeds in his garden, tends them lovingly, and when they "bring forth" as he planned, sees to it that they are fed and protected, and that if something goes wrong, it is corrected.

One of the reasons God created human beings was to help take care of the creation on the earth, and see to it that it brought forth properly. That's why a human being is both spiritual and physical, able to live on the earth and also to have fellowship with God in the spiritual world. Even the pagan philosophers believed human beings were mixtures of spiritual and material.[8]

The Scripture record makes it clear that human beings were specially created by God. They were not just "brought forth" by the earth and water. In Genesis, after the other living things have been "brought forth," there is a pause in the creation story and God says, "Let Us make man in Our image." (The "image of God" is, of course, a spiritual image not a physical one. We are made like Him spiritually so we can choose to respond to Him and have fellowship with Him.) Then, says the Scripture, "God made man from the dust of the earth, breathed into his nostrils a spirit (breath) of life, and man became a living being."[9] The earth could not "bring forth" the human spirit. The human spirit is not "developed." It is directly created by God. It doesn't come from the physical world.

But what about the "dust of the earth," the body into which God put the human spirit? Might He not have allowed the earth to "bring forth" and develop the pre-human body until it was ready to carry the complexity of human reason, and ready to house the human spirit? Is there anything unscriptural in this, provided we make it clear that man's *spirit* is a special creation? If God created man to be a bridge between the spiritual world and the material world, would it not make sense for man's body to be taken from the earth in every sense of the word? Paul says, "The first man is of the earth, earthy."[10] It does answer a lot of awkward questions. Why is my body so similar to the animals? Why do I have the same basic bone structure as the higher vertebrates? Why do I have vestigial organs and structures, such as the vermiform appendix and the coccyx, that would indicate development from pre-human forms?

C. S. Lewis, a man whose writings have meant a great deal to me, as to so many others, seemed to have believed God went about it in this way. In his well-known space trilogy, he imagines the Green Lady and her husband on the planet Perelandra to have come physically from the sea. He pictures a kind of creature living in the water which is clearly a subrational species.[11] In the first novel of the series, *Out of the Silent Planet,* his hero discovers that on the planet Malacandra (Mars), three species have "reached rationality," that is, developed to the point where God could give them spirits.[12] Yet no one who knows his work would accuse Dr. Lewis of not respecting the Scripture, or of not being a fully-believing Christian. In fact, he has become something of a hero in conservative Christian circles because of his tremendously logical and clear way of presenting and defending basic Christian faith. I'm not saying Dr. Lewis was right, but what he thought about creation seems not to have affected his credibility in orthodox Christian circles. (On the other hand, in his outstanding series of children's stories, *The Chronicles of Narnia,* Lewis beautifully portrays the instantaneous creation of a world, although even there he imagines the "earth bringing forth" the creatures in response to Aslan's song.)[13]

I do not think we can begin to imagine what those first human beings were like—the change which the incoming of the human spirit, in the image of God, made in the earthy body into which it was placed. What was the human physical body like when it was completely under the control of the unfallen human spirit, and completely in contact with God? It may be that all the natural processes which we think are normal to human beings, such as eating and eliminating wastes, and other bodily processes, are really subnormal, things that became necessary when the human spirit lost fellowship with God, and lost control of the physical body, which then lapsed back to a more animal-like way of living.

We have evidence that people can live without food, or with an absolute minimum of food, when they are especially inspired by the Spirit of God. It was claimed that Theresa Neumann of Bavaria lived for many years on no other food but the tiny morsel of bread she received daily in Holy Communion.[14] St. Catherine of Siena is reported to have lived for a long period in the same fashion. A friend told how, when he was a captain in the army in World War II, his outfit had been stranded without supplies. He went away from the encampment to pray and felt that he had suddenly been miraculously fed, so that when he returned to his command, his other officers asked him, "Where did you get the food?" It is a common experience for people to feel no need of sleep or food during periods of great spiritual inspiration. It is quite conceivable that God can minister life directly to the human body, when He has full access to the human spirit.

So God gave man full power and authority over the creation on this earth, to "dress it and keep it"—that is, take care of it, and make it more beautiful. But human beings allowed the authority to fall into the hands of our spiritual enemy, Satan. The result was that not only was God cut off from man, but His tending and care of the rest of the earth was seriously interfered with, if not halted. We have said that entropy is the basic law of the physical world, that things will run down into greater and greater confusion unless there is someone organizing and ordering them. But the organizer has to stay on the job, because the minute his influence is removed, the running down begins again. My garage only stays neat if I keep putting things away and cleaning things up. Just one clean-up won't do. The minute I stop, it begins deteriorating into a mess again.

So you can see when God's loving care of His creation was interfered with or interrupted by man's fall, disorder began to take over again. Not only that, since this world had come under the power of the "rulers of the darkness," they seized every opportunity to introduce further confusion and destruction into the scene.

This helps to answer other difficult questions. Where do the "evil beasts," as the Bible calls them, come from? Why is nature so cruel, as well as so beautiful? Why were there species which seemed to go off into dead ends? Why is there such a confusion of species?

Evolution in the Headlines

Evolution is in the headlines again. In 1982 a federal judge declared unconstitutional an Arkansas statute insisting on equal time for the teaching of both evolution and the biblical version of creation in the schools. The judge said this was a violation of church-state separation, since the biblical version of creation was religious teaching.

We can't blame the judge for his decision. Christianity enjoys no special privileges in our country; in fact, if anything, it is discriminated against. Then, too, if Christian beliefs were allowed to be taught in public schools, the other religions would certainly insist on equal time for their teachings.

The attempts to get a literal version of the Genesis creation taught as science in the nation's schools are doomed to failure from the start. Genesis is not science, it is faith—it is revelation. It involves a particular belief about the nature of God.

The first question isn't *how* God created the world, or how long it took Him. The first question is whether God, as the supreme Source of intelligence and meaning, was present at the very beginning, and created everything, or whether it all happened by accident. The most important passage in Genesis is the first one: "In the beginning

God created the heavens and the earth." If God comes first—if the first Truth is a Personal Being—then everything else falls into place. You can discuss the "how" of it later. If we limit ourselves to this question, we have a battle we can win. *And the concept of a Creator can be taught as science.*

Schoolteachers cannot legally teach belief in the Genesis version of creation, but we can insist that they teach that the world did not come about by accident, but was created. Christians have strangely overlooked the fact that the first of the documents upon which our republic is founded, the Declaration of Independence, states that men are "endowed by their Creator with certain unalienable Rights...." Thus, not only can it be taught in public schools that there is a Creator; the case can be made that to teach that the world came about by accident destroys the very basis for human rights on which our nation is founded!

We can legally insist that our children have a right to be taught in public school that the world was created by a Creator; it did not come about by blind chance. If this point is made, the other questions of "how" and "when" can be dealt with at home and in church. I don't mean to say that a simple belief in God as Creator is sufficient. The only ultimate hope for the United States, or any other nation, is to acknowledge Jesus Christ as Lord; but the teaching of God as Creator leaves the door open for the gospel, whereas in the present situation our children are conditioned against belief in God by the teaching that the world came about by accident.

It's Scientific to Teach Creation

You see, belief in a Creator *can* be taught as an impersonal scientific fact. It does not necessarily involve personal faith. The *nature* of the Creator is a matter of personal faith, but His existence is not. What many Christians are slow to appreciate is that scientists who are truly on the frontiers are more and more questioning the validity of "accidentalism." Sir Fred Hoyle, leading English physicist and cosmologist, says in a recent book, "Biochemical systems are exceedingly complex, so much so that the chance of their being formed through random shufflings of simple organic molecules is exceedingly minute, to a point indeed where it is insensibly different from zero."[15] Scientists are beginning more and more to admit that it's impossible for the world to have come into existence by accident, and that they simply don't know how it all came about.

Dr. Hoyle says, "From the beginning of this book we have emphasized the enormous information content of even the simplest living systems. The information cannot in our view be generated by what are often called 'natural' processes. . . . We have argued that the requisite information came from an 'intelligence'. . . ."

Richard de Mille, in an unusual article in the *National Review,* says that scientists,

have publicly clung to and incoherently defended a moribund explanation of how evolution occurs—the neo-Darwinian interpretation, which tries to explain new species solely in terms of the selection of accidental genetic variations by environmental pressures. It just doesn't work. Bonnie and Clyde's last ride was nothing compared with the holes that have been shot through neo-Darwinian natural selection. Darwin himself was plenty worried about it. How, he wondered, could something as complicated as the human eye evolve by tiny adaptive steps, when it couldn't serve any adaptive purpose until it was fully evolved? Many evolutionary marvels (said Norman Macbeth, in *Darwin Retried*) are not adaptations at all; they are *works of art.** In 1966, a band of upstart mathematicians argued effectively that the genetic odds must crush accidental evolution; *some undiscovered principle, they said, must be directing genetic variations. . . .* If Darwin *is* being discarded (said Tom Bethell in *Harper's,* February 1976—an article I recommend), "it is being done as discreetly and gently as possible with a minimum of publicity." Yes indeed, and the highschool textbook writers have not been let in on the secret. [*Italics mine.][16]

You see, secular thinkers are beginning to see the accidental theory just won't wash, it just won't do. What is the alternative? Mr. de Mille is frank about it. At the outset he says,

Three alternatives remain: God created the world in six days; the universe and everything in it happened by accident; or we haven't a clue to the origin, destiny, or purpose of existence.

He says he is a subscriber to the third alternative, but at the end of the article he says,

Compromise is possible here, but each side has to give something up. The scientists have to give up their ragged Darwinian security blanket and confess that they simply don't know how evolution occurs. The Creationists have to give up just enough of their rigid literalism to allow God room to move in a mysterious way, His evolution to perform. If both sides can do that, science, religion, and education will all be better for it.

Statements like Dr. Hoyle's, and articles like de Mille's, show that the doors are opening to reestablish communication between Christians and the scientific community. Science is moving away from materialism, as anyone familiar with happenings on the frontiers of quantum mechanics will certainly appreciate. I certainly don't agree with everything in the de Mille article, but I am saying that now is the time for Christians to provide intelligent input, not ill-tempered argument and condemnation. If we don't provide it, scientists will look elsewhere for answers, and will turn to the psychic and occult, as some are already doing—and the last state may be worse than the first!

We Must Close the Generation Gap

In Malachi 4, God predicts that the heart of the fathers shall be turned to the children, and the heart of the children to their fathers.

Your children are taught, not only in school, but in the books they read and the programs they watch on TV that they and the world they live in came about by accident.

When your kids go to Sunday School, however, they are told, "God made you," the implication being that God put them together much the way they build things with their construction sets. That sounds real good, for healthy kids. But what does it say to a youngster who was born with a defective body? Doesn't God know what He is doing? Does He sometimes make mistakes or leave things out when He puts people together?

Your kids may be able to survive this contradiction in grade school, or even through high school, but when they get to college the chances are they will decide what they were told in church about creation was a fairy tale, and therefore the rest of their religious teaching may have been too. Then you will hear the parent say something like, "Oh, our son has started college, and some terrible professor has got to him, and he's just *lost* his faith!"

If you want to reach your children, and your friends, too, you should not pick a quarrel with science, which has such tremendous credibility in the modern world. Kids are fascinated by dinosaurs and tales of prehistoric times. Are you going to tell them these things did not exist? That all the books they read and things they hear about them are just fairy stories? Your child is much more likely to dismiss *you* as the teller of fairy tales! Don't give your children, or your friends, reason to turn you off, as old-fashioned and uninformed. You will do better to concede to your children and friends that much of what they are told by the scientific world is true, but then point out to them that without a Creator it would be both ridiculous and impossible. Keep the lines of communication open, and the more you can accept and understand what they already believe, the better, provided you do not compromise your own faith.

Christians should not argue before the world about the method God used, or how long He took. That's family stuff. We can discuss it, in love, if we want to. To the world we should be maintaining that there is a Creator, that that is a scientific fact which does not depend on special revelation or a special kind of faith, that there is hard scientific evidence of an Intelligence behind the creation. It could not have come about without a Planner, an Organizer.

We who believe in and know God have got to stop retreating before materialism, and show how science and faith are related.

Begin at the Right End

I believe in God because I have met Him. No matter what supposed scientific evidence was given me to the contrary, I could never be convinced any other way, any more than you could convince me that there is no sky over my head. F. W. H. Myers said:

Whoso has felt the Spirit of the Highest
Cannot confound, nor doubt Him, nor deny:
Yea, with one voice, O world, though thou deniest,
Stand thou on that side, for on this am I.[17]

There are a lot of people, though, who want to believe, but they can't, because they are blocked by their intellects. They need to get answers. Let's clear away the popular misconceptions that keep people from believing. I'm not passing any judgment here on the question of whether the earth was created in six solar days, or in six ages, or periods of time, as many Christians would interpret it. I am saying that to win the battle in the public schools, we must set those questions aside and focus on the heart of the matter which I have tried to set forth.

I have no difficulty in accepting that God could have created the world in six days, or six seconds, or six billion years. He is God. He is outside the limitations of space and time. But people who haven't yet come to know Him can only be expected to follow the internal evidence of the world we live in. If you accept divine revelation, in the Bible and in your life, God can tell you things you couldn't find out by scientific investigation of the world from inside it. But He has still left clues in the world for those who want to believe. We can begin by pointing out those clues, and so lead people to meet Him, and know Him, and understand more clearly what He has done, and what He is doing.

Finally, the most important thing is that we love, and not judge, one another. We may not find out the total answer to such mysteries in this life, but when we're with Jesus face to face He can then say to us, "Confidentially, my child, this is the way I did it." We'll probably all be surprised!

Notes

1. *Time,* May 25, 1953, p. 82.
2. *Encyclopedia Brittanica,* 1974 Edition, Vol. X, p. 901c.
3. Rifkin, *Entropy,* p. 6.
4. Genesis 1:2.
5. It's interesting that Genesis describes the birds as coming from the *waters.* Paleontologists surmise that birds developed from reptiles, which are basically water creatures.
6. Webster's *New Collegiate Dictionary* (Springfield, Mass.: Merriam, 1980), p. 393.
7. Matthew 8:27.
8. Some of the great pagan philosophers thought so too, For example, in the *Timaeus,* Plato represents man as being given a share in the divine nature. He describes the "creator of the universe" speaking to the lesser gods, and telling them they are to create mortal beings which he himself will endow with spirits, saying, "ye yourselves interweave the mortal with the immortal." Plato, *Timaeus,* Jowett Translation (University of Chicago, 1952).
9. Genesis 2:7 paraphrased.
10. 1 Corinthians 15:47.
11. Lewis, *Perelandra,* p. 102.
12. Lewis, *Out of the Silent Planet,* p. 72.
13. Lewis, *The Magician's Nephew,* pp. 100–102.
14. *Encyclopedia Brittanica,* 1973, Vol. VII, p. 275.
15. (F. Hoyle and N.C. Wickramasinghe, *Evolution from Space* (London: J. M. Dent & Sons, 1981) pp. 3, 150.
16. Richard de Mille, "And God Created Evolution," *National Review,* March 19, 1982, pp. 288, 292.
17. F. W. H. Myers, *The Inner Light.*

8

Falling Under the Power

In Christian history, whenever the Holy Spirit has been moving strongly, some people have "gone down under the power," that is to say, they have fallen down, overwhelmed by the presence of God. Great revivalists such as Wesley and Finney noted this happening in their meetings. It was common during the Great Awakening in the United States in the eighteenth century.

In the early days of the Pentecostal revival, people often fell "under the power."* It is told that at the great Azusa Street meeting in 1906 people would be overwhelmed by God's presence and fall to the floor as soon as they came into the building.

In more recent times, Gerald Derstine, for example, tells how one of the first signs of a fresh moving of the Holy Spirit in his very reserved Mennonite congregation was that a number of young people fell out of their chairs![1]

---

* It is commonly termed being "slain in the spirit," but I don't think this is a good name for it. The term seems to have been taken from Isaiah 66:16, which says "the slain of the Lord shall be many." Presumably the person who selected this Scripture to validate the experience had not read the context. It isn't speaking of a blessing from God, but of the destruction of His enemies!

Is this a valid manifestation of the Spirit of God, or is it simply emotionalism?

It would be easy to dismiss it as mere emotionalism. The psychological suggestion is often obvious: a strong build-up ahead of time to get people to expect to fall; men standing behind waiting to catch them. Sometimes blankets are piled waiting to throw over the ladies in the interest of modesty. I've seen people fall down obviously just to cooperate. I once saw an elderly lady go down holding on to her hat! Sometimes it seems, too, that the evangelist gives a little extra push!

Yet it's happening today in churches that could hardly be called emotionalistic, such as the Anglican (Episcopal) and Roman. The Roman Catholics call it "resting in the Spirit." It isn't new, even there. More than fifteen years ago, when the charismatic renewal was just beginning in the Episcopal Church, I heard a woman complain: "As I was kneeling at the altar rail, waiting to be confirmed, the bishop laid his hands on the woman kneeling next to me and she fell right over on me!"

Shortly after I came to St. Luke's Episcopal Church in Seattle, one Thursday morning two of my parishioners, women in middle life, were kneeling at the altar rail following a communion service. They both wanted prayer for healing. I laid my hands on each of them in turn and prayed for them, then moved on to pray for others. Afterward the two came to me: "What's going on?" they asked. "When you prayed for us just now we both nearly fell over! We would have, if we hadn't been propped up against the altar rail!"

As far as I know these women knew nothing about the phenomenon of falling under the power, and I didn't either.

Much more recently, perhaps four years ago, following a meeting in a Presbyterian church in Idaho, Rita prayed with some fifty people to receive freedom in the Holy Spirit. A man in the group, an architect, began to prophesy.* While he was speaking, two elderly

---

* "Prophecy" is one of the gifts of the Spirit. It doesn't necessarily mean foretelling the future. It means "forthtelling," that is, speaking out words from the Lord. The key phrase for prophecy is, "thus says the Lord." Paul says it's for "edification, exhortation, and comfort." Moses and Paul both said they wished all of God's people would prophesy (Numbers 11:29; 1 Corinthians 14:5, 24, 31).

ladies went sailing to the floor as lightly as you please, apparently overcome by the glory of the Lord.

We were praying for people in an Episcopal cathedral in the Southeast. A man who had just experienced the release of the Holy Spirit got up from the altar rail, took a few steps, but again fell to his knees because he couldn't stand up!

Rita prayed for a woman at a retreat in Oklahoma who then had to be carried to her room because her legs just wouldn't hold her up. She remained caught up in the Spirit all night and in the morning found that she had been healed of a painful neuritis.

In California, a 92-year-old-man, after being prayed with for the release of the Holy Spirit, found himself on the floor. People were naturally concerned over his condition, but he was fine. He stayed there about an hour and then got up and went home. He was at church, bright and cheery, the next morning.

In none of these cases was there any attempt to work people up or to condition them by suggestion. The "fallings" were entirely spontaneous and unexpected, both to us and to the people themselves. They did not seem to be emotional reactions, but responses to the Spirit of God.

What Does it Mean?

What is this "falling under the power"? Does it have any real significance or purpose in the spiritual life?

The Lord doesn't knock His faithful people down. This isn't something He's doing, but the human body and soul sometimes respond to the moving of the Holy Spirit in this way, suddenly losing muscle tone and strength, totally relaxing and letting go, so that the person collapses to the floor. Someone described it as falling in a "happy little heap"! The person does not lose consciousness; he or she is just overwhelmed by the love and glory of God. Most people say they are greatly refreshed by the experience. They'll often say something like, "I felt as though I spent a little time in heaven with the Lord."

"Falling under the power" can happen sometimes to very solid and stable Christians, often without them previously knowing anything about it. If you consistently pray with and for others you know that people respond this way from time to time.

Is It Scriptural?

Is it scriptural? It would seem so. Twice the Scripture says of Ezekiel that when he saw God's glory, he fell on his face (Ezekiel 1:28; 3:23). John the apostle saw the glorified Jesus and "fell at his feet as one dead."[2] Daniel was visited by the archangel Gabriel and the Hebrew says he was "stupified" or "stunned."[3] This happened again, where Daniel says as he saw the vision "what strength I had deserted me."[4] The same sort of thing seems to have happened to Abraham when God was sealing the covenant with him.[5] At the consecration of Solomon's temple, 2 Chronicles 5:14 says "the priests could not stand to minister by reason of the cloud: for the glory of the Lord had filled the house of God." The Hebrew here can mean many things: stand, endure, remain. Many scholars would say the verse just means the priests were overwhelmed by awe and fear. We are not told, though, that they ran away, so we may presume they simply fell down, literally unable to "stand" in the presence of God's glory.

On the Day of Pentecost, the disciples were accused of being drunk. This was another example of men and women being unable to stand up because they were overcome by the glory.

Yes, there is no doubt but that the Bible tells of people "falling under the power." Note, however, that no one laid hands on Daniel or John or the priests in Solomon's temple, in order for them to fall down. They fell down because they were overwhelmed by God's presence just as people seem to have done in the times of spiritual outpouring in Christian history. The Wesleys, or Mr. Finney, were not trying to get people to fall down in their meetings; in fact, the Wesleys in particular must have rather wished that kind of thing wouldn't happen. John was having enough trouble dealing with the complacent and corrupt church of the day, without having to explain why people sometimes fell down when he preached to them!

We can find no example in the Bible of someone having been touched or had hands laid on him to cause him to fall under the power. Nevertheless, it is true that people do fall sometimes when hands are laid on them. Part of this may be simple psychological suggestion, but it is certainly true that the power of the Holy Spirit can move through the hands of a person who is indwelt by the Spirit, and that means any Christian. I have had someone say, when I laid my hands on her for healing, "Oh, you're burning me!" I didn't feel the heat of the Spirit, but she did. Rita tells how when she was seeking to understand better the meaning of the ministry of the Holy Spirit, and was standing praying in a circle with others, holding hands, suddenly a jolt like electricity went through her. No one else in the circle felt it.

A Change of Emphasis

"Falling under the power" certainly happened a good deal in the early days of the Pentecostal revival, but we don't hear of the great pioneers of the Pentecostal renewal, like Smith Wigglesworth, emphasizing it. It happened, but it happened spontaneously, and was taken for granted as a sign of the power of the Spirit. They didn't focus on it. It's a heady thing, though, to have people fall down when you lay hands on them; and it's easy to persuade yourself, and others, that the reason they fall down is that you have special power. So gradually there came a change. Some evangelists began to make it a regular pattern in their ministry that when they prayed with people, they fell down. People were encouraged by teaching and example to expect it to happen.

The phenomenon was featured in the ministry of the late Kathryn Kuhlman, and many have followed her example. It is common to find evangelists and teachers at conferences today encouraging people to fall under the power. Sometimes it seems to be a build-up of prestige for the evangelist, which is a far cry from someone spontaneously falling before the glory of God. A couple of years ago I read the publicity statements of a minister who claimed when he pointed at people they would fall down. Another said all he had to do was blow his breath at them! Still another would lay hands on the same person several times, to make him or her repeatedly fall down, or would touch people suddenly from behind to make them fall. The element of suggestion seems clear enough in these last examples.

Falling and Healing

Anyone with a public ministry knows that people's responses will ebb and flow. Sometimes they seem ready and open to believe and receive, and sometimes not. Falling under the power seems to provide a convenient way of demonstrating that the Lord is honoring the ministry. And since people do receive God's blessings when they are open and ready to believe, healings and other answers to prayer sometimes take place concurrently with the person falling under the power. In other words, the person is open both to be healed, and to fall under the power, and there is no doubt that the complete, physical letting-go in the falling, helps the person to be open and non-resisting to the ministry of healing. The impression is sometimes given, though, that the healing *came* through falling under the power. Folks get the idea, "this is the way you do it. If I can just fall down, I will get help—healing, the baptism in the Holy Spirit, the faith and strength I need."

Though people may be healed during an experience of falling under the power, they have as often not been. If a person goes down expecting to be healed and it doesn't happen, he may be discouraged, thinking "if *that* didn't work, nothing will!" Or if he does not fall he may think, "Oh dear, I'm just not yielded enough!" Yet dramatic healings can take place with no outward manifestation or feeling at all. Indeed sometimes people will be healed hours or even days after being prayed with. In my first eight years as pastor of St. Luke's we had striking examples of healing and other miracles, but (outside of those first two ladies I told about) no example of anyone falling under the power. It's never a good idea to base your faith on outward signs. "Christians don't follow signs; signs follow Christians!"

Kathryn Kuhlman did not urge falling under the power as a means for healing. She would encourage people to trust God for their healing while sitting in the meeting and sought to strengthen their faith through the gifts of knowledge: "Someone over there is being healed of arthritis," she would say, or "A woman in the right balcony just received a healing of her back." People would release their faith and the Lord would heal them right there. Many thousands were healed this way through Kathryn's ministry. She would call them to come forward and testify *after* they had been healed, and at that time she customarily laid hands on them to fall under the power. The healing had already taken place.

Not only is the experience of falling under the power mistakenly used to prove the holiness and power of the evangelist and the validity of his or her ministry, it is also thought to prove that the person falling is specially submissive to the Spirit of God. Gwen, a fine Christian woman, says to her friends: "If you haven't gone down under the power, you just aren't yielded to the Lord!"

This encourages people to think that being "yielded to the Lord" means being passive. A lot of folk would like to have something done to them which would solve their problems without effort on their part, perhaps through deliverance, or by someone getting them to fall under the power. It's always spiritually and psychologically dangerous to be passive, because that means you're open to whatever comes along. Some need, not to fall down under the power, but to repent and forgive, change their attitudes, and be healed in their souls.

Here is Ben, a young clergyman of a historic denomination, who says that everyone needs to be "slain in the spirit" at least once a week, in order to keep free and fresh! Yet Ben's friends know that he himself has deep problems that he is refusing to face and that his personal life is seriously out of line. He seems to be trying to maintain a spiritual "high" by external means, instead of coming to grips with his need for emotional healing.

Other Reasons for Falling

Falling down supernaturally isn't always a sign that people are receiving a blessing. We need to be aware that there are at least two other reasons why they may fall down.

People may fall down because they are in rebellion against God. Paul was thrown down on the Damascus road at the time of his conversion,[6] and the men who came to arrest Jesus fell backward to the ground.[7] In both these cases, those who fell were enemies of the Lord at the time. Paul was knocked down and temporarily blinded by the Spirit in order to humble him and confront him with Jesus. The men coming to arrest Jesus were thrown backward to the ground by just a glimpse of His real power and glory. Jesus perhaps did this to remind His disciples He was still in full command of the situation, even though He was allowing Himself to be arrested.

So, unbelievers today may fall down in God's presence, then they may either yield to Him and be converted as was Paul, or they may continue to resist for the time, as did the soldiers who arrested Jesus.

Secondly, some people may fall because they are being troubled by an evil spirit. We have grown more cautious in recent days, but before we learned better we used to sometimes overlook the warning of the Apostle Paul and "lay hands suddenly" on someone who asked for prayer, without first finding out his or her spiritual condition.[8] The result was that now and then a person would fall and thrash about, and behave in a highly abnormal and disturbing way, because he or she was in fact oppressed by an evil spirit. This may be one of the reasons the early Pentecostals were nicknamed "Holy Rollers." They were pioneers in a new dimension and were not always cautious in praying with people. Occasionally someone would indeed roll, and go through various other gyrations. When people are having hands laid on them "suddenly," especially in large meetings, without their spiritual condition being known, some among them who may need deliverance may be treated as if they were just "getting a blessing."

In his book, *Spiritual Warfare,* Michael Harper tells how in

England in 1965, following a meeting, he and I were praying with a group of people to receive the baptism in the Holy Spirit. Everyone was very quiet and proper. I came to a young man whose round collar showed he was a minister. I had barely touched him when he fell to the floor as if he had been thrown down. He was obviously in great distress. The others who were helping me took the man into the main hall. There, after he was thrown down a second time, they were able to cast out the spirits that were tormenting him and the young clergyman went home happy, praising God, much different than the way he had come.[9]

The presence of the Holy Spirit may stir up a rebellious spirit to such grotesque actions, and then when the evil spirit is rebuked in the Name of Jesus, the person will sometimes pass right out and may remain unconscious for some time. In Mark 9:14–27, Jesus cast out an evil spirit which had caused a child to be unable to hear or speak. When Jesus cast out the spirit, the child fell down as if he were dead, but Jesus took him by the hand and lifted him to his feet. He was perfectly cured.

The Balanced Viewpoint

People are going to fall in the Spirit from time to time when they are prayed with, and real benefits may accompany the experience. It should not be emphasized, though, as necessary to healing or any other of God's blessings, nor as signifying special power or yieldedness. People should not be encouraged to "follow the leader," which they are only too quick to do. The Lord is a God of variety, and different people respond differently to His presence and power.

Back in 1970, our good friend and former secretary, Janet Koether, was struggling to grasp what it meant when this manifestation began to be so popular. She felt God gave her an illustration:

> I searched the Bible, asking the Lord about it. I had become quite distressed with what I felt were excesses and a preoccupation with "going down under the power," on the part of many

Christians. Sort of like this was the newest toy, and you just weren't "with it" unless you had been "slain in the Spirit."

One day, while I was driving my car, I cried out to the Lord to give me an answer and help me have peace about it. It was then that I saw (in the Spirit) a beautiful mountain scene in the summer time. There was a large, refreshing waterfall of the most clear, pure water I had ever seen. Then I noticed there were people of all ages around the waterfall, enjoying themselves. Some were splashing in it; others were edging up as close as they dared to the base of the falls, letting the water splash on them. Others were climbing part-way up the side of the lush, green mountain and riding down the rushing water, like going down a slide. After reaching the bottom, they would go back up for another ride.

Then I looked out beyond the waterfall and to my amazement saw a vast brown desert, with huge cracks in it which went on as far as I could see. What amazed me was that there was all this water; but for some reason, it wasn't getting out to the parched desert. I asked the Lord why, and He showed me He is a powerful God and has living water for His children to refresh them. It's good that they should be blessed and refreshed. He is very powerful, and when they "climb up the waterfall" they do fall down because of the sheer power of the water. Thinking this is great fun, they climb up the waterfall over and over again, making a game of it. As I looked at the people playing around the waterfall, I noticed that they were so preoccupied with the fun they were having, they didn't see the parched desert!

The Lord then showed me that He desires the refreshing, living water of His Spirit to be taken out into the desert to nourish and bless it, but the water has to be taken there *by His children.* His children need to be blessed and refreshed, too, but they should not just make a game of playing with His power, but take His Living Water out into the desert so that all the people of the earth can be blessed. With this I felt the peace of God once more.

Shortly after I had been baptized in the Holy Spirit, I was conducting a communion service in my church in Van Nuys, California. As I turned from the altar to face the people what I can only describe as a "wave of love and fellowship" flowed up to me from the congregation, many of whom had been newly released in the Holy Spirit.

This was at a very solemn point of the Liturgy—the invitation to prepare for Holy Communion by confession of sin—but I felt that I either had to shout "praise the Lord" or I would fall to the floor from the sheer weight of the love. I knew that neither action would be in order at that time, so I controlled myself and went on with the service!

You may at some time feel the overwhelming presence of God when you know that for you to fall under the power would be quite out of order. You need to realize that God will bless and be with you whether you fall or stand. Second Corinthians 5:13 describes it well: "Whether we be beside ourselves, it is to God; or whether we be sober, it is for your cause."

There are Scriptures which tell us we must be born again and bear fruit, and that we must receive the power of the Spirit with His gifts, but there aren't any which say Christians must fall down under God's power. So if it hasn't happened to you, don't feel you've missed out. Some have this experience and some do not, not because they are unyielded or unspiritual, but simply because their physical and emotional makeup is such that they don't respond that way. The Spirit of God shows Himself in different modes. Paul had visions, Peter walked on the water, Enoch and Elijah were carried up bodily into heaven, Philip was transported many miles in the Spirit. The important thing is to be doing God's will day by day. If the Lord wants to give you a vision, He will, but you may get in trouble if you sit around praying for or trying to manufacture one! Whatever supernatural blessings the Lord has for us, let's be open to them, but not force others into our mold nor deny God's unique dealings in their lives. Above all, let's take the Living Water out into the dry parched world we live in.

Notes

1. Derstine, *Following the Fire.*
2. Revelation 1:17.
3. Daniel 8:17, 18.
4. Daniel 10:8 Jerusalem Bible.
5. Genesis 15:12.
6. Acts 9:4.
7. John 18:16.
8. 1 Timothy 5:22.
9. Michael Harper, *Spiritual Warfare* (London: Hodder and Stoughton, 1970), pp. 11–13.

Bibliography

Bennett, Dennis, *Nine O'Clock in the Morning* (Plainfield, N.J.: Logos, 1970).

Bennett, Dennis and Rita, *The Holy Spirit and You* (Plainfield, N.J.: Logos, 1971).

————, *Trinity of Man* (Plainfield, N.J.: Logos, 1979).

Derstine, Gerald with Joanne Derstine Layman. *Following the Fire* (Plainfield, N.J.: Logos, 1980).

Frodsham, Stanley H., *Smith Wigglesworth: Apostle of Faith* (London: Assemblies of God Publishing House, 1948).

Gross, Don H., *The Case for Spiritual Healing* (New York: Nelson, 1958).

Latourette, Kenneth S., *A History of Christianity*, Vols. 1 and 2 (New York: Harper and Row, 1975).

Lewis, C. S., *Mere Christianity* (New York: Macmillan, reprint 1977).

————, *Out of the Silent Planet* (New York: Macmillan, reprint 1971).

————, *Perelandra* (New York: Macmillan, 1968).

————, *The Magician's Nephew* (New York: Macmillan, 1955).

————, *The Pilgrim's Regress* (New York: Bantam, 1981).

Neal, Emily G., *A Reporter Finds God Through Spiritual Healing* (New York: Morehouse-Gorham, 1956).

————, *The Lord Is Our Healer* (Englewood Cliffs, N.J.: Prentice-Hall, 1961).

Reed, William S., *Healing the Whole Man,* formerly *Surgery of the Soul* (Plainfield, N.J.: Logos, 1969).

Rifkin, Jeremy, *Entropy* (New York: Viking, 1980).

Sanford, Agnes, *Sealed Orders* (Plainfield, N.J.: Logos, 1972). *The Healing Light* (St. Paul, Minn.: Macalester, 1947).

Wesley, John, *The Journal of John Wesley* (Chicago: Moody, 1952).

Wigglesworth, Smith, *Ever Increasing Faith* (Springfield, Mo: Gospel Publishing House, 1924).

Other Books on Healing

Bennett, Rita M., *Emotionally Free* (Old Tappan, N.J.: Revell, 1982).

Bosworth, F. F., *Christ the Healer* (Old Tappan, N.J.: Revell, 1973).

Large, John E., *The Ministry of Healing* (New York: Morehouse-Gorham, 1959).

Murray, Andrew, *Divine Healing* (Plainfield, N.J.: Logos, 1974).